GS SCORE

AN INSTITUTE FOR CIVIL SERVICES

STATE OF INDIAN ECONOMY

STATE OF INDIAN ECONOMY

EDITED BY

MANOJ K. JHA & SUBHANJANI YADAV

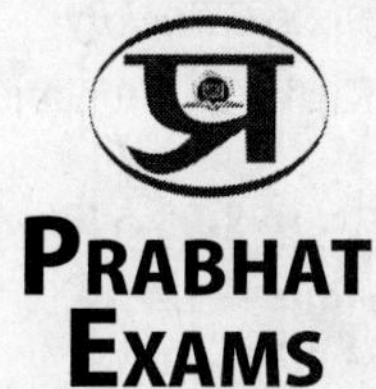

PRABHAT EXAMS

Publisher

PRABHAT EXAMS

Imprint of Prabhat Prakashan Pvt. Ltd.

4/19 Asaf Ali Road, New Delhi–110 002

Ph. 23289555 • 23289666 • 23289777 • Helpline/ 7827007777

e-mail: prabhatbooks@gmail.com • Website: www.prabhatexam.com

Price

Three Hundred Ninety Five Rupees

ISBN 978-93-5488-804-5

Printed at

Nakshatra Art, Delhi

GSSCORE

STATE OF INDIAN ECONOMY

Edited by

Manoj K. Jha & Subhanjani Yadav

ISBN 978-93-5488-804-5

₹ 395.00

Editorial Team

The Economic Survey of India and Union Budget are of great significance for the Civil Services Examination as direct questions are asked from this segment. In the examination, roughly half of the 15-20 economics-related questions pertain to information from the Economic Survey and Budget.

Its significance extends beyond the corridors of governance, reaching the desks of aspirants preparing for competitive examinations. Recognizing the paramount importance of these documents, this book offers a distilled essence—

- **A concise summary** of the 'The Indian Economy: A Review; Interim Budget & Previous Years' Economic Survey' to give the reader the important information from the original text while ensuring that it is concise yet clear.
- **Important terminologies** to enable readers to simplify and understand the document.
- **Value addition** to enable aspirants to build the correct narrative and add to their knowledge.
- **A thorough analysis** of budgets and surveys offers valuable insights into financial dynamics and societal trends.
- **Practice Questions** (for both Prelims and Mains) to validate one's learning.

It is sincerely hoped that the summarisation add to your preparation and serve as your compass, helping you understand India's economy better and boosting your success in exams.

*****

CONTENT

THE INDIAN ECONOMY: A REVIEW

KEY-TERMS

- **Fiscal Deficit:**

  It is the difference between a government's total revenue and its total expenditure, excluding money from borrowings; an indicator of the government's borrowing requirements.

- **Current Account Deficit:**

  Current Account Deficit (CAD) occurs when a country's total imports of goods, services, and transfers exceed its total exports. It reflects a negative balance in the current account of the balance of payments. A persistent CAD may indicate dependency on foreign financing and potential economic imbalances.

- **Twin Deficit:**

  Twin deficit refer to fiscal and current account deficit. It is a combined shortfall between a country's government revenues and its export income.

- **Revenue Deficit:**

  If the balance of total revenue receipts and total revenue expenditures turns out to be negative it is known as revenue deficit.

- **Effective Revenue Deficit:**

  Effective Revenue Deficit (ERD) is a new term introduced in the Union Budget 2011–12. Revenue Expenditures includes all the grants which the Union Government gives to the state governments and the UTs—some of which create assets. ERD is the RD 'excluding' those revenue expenditures of the Government of India which were done in the form of GoCA (grants for creation of capital assets).

- **Primary Deficit:**

  It is simply the fiscal deficit minus the interest payments.

- **Gross Fiscal Deficit (GFD):**

  It is the excess of total expenditure including loans net of recovery over revenue receipts (including external grants) and non-debt capital receipts. The net fiscal deficit is the gross fiscal deficit less net lending of the Central government.

- **Inflation:**

  Inflation is the sustained increase in the general price level of goods and services in an economy over time. It erodes the purchasing power of a currency, reducing the amount of goods and services that can be bought with the same amount of money. Central banks often aim to maintain a target inflation rate to ensure price stability and economic growth.

- **Devaluation:**

  Devaluation is the deliberate downward adjustment to the value of a country's currency relative to another currency or standard.

- **Gross Tax Revenue:**

  The total revenue collected by the government through various taxes before deducting refunds or other adjustments.

- **Goods and Services Tax (GST):**

  A unified indirect tax levied on the supply of goods and services, aimed at simplifying the tax structure and promoting a common market.

- **Disinvestment:**

  It is the process of selling government-owned assets, shares, or stakes in public enterprises to private investors.

- **Non-Debt Capital Receipts:**

  Receipts that do not create a liability for the government in the form of debt, often including proceeds from asset sales or recovery of loans. Examples: Sale of government-owned assets, recovery of loans, or dividends from state-owned enterprises.

- **Capital expenditure:**

  Capital expenditures (CapEx) are funds used by a company to acquire, upgrade, and maintain physical assets such as property, plants, buildings, technology, or equipment.

- **Government Securities (G-Sec) Market:**

  A Government Security (G-Sec) is a tradeable instrument issued by the Central Government or the State Governments. It acknowledges the Government's debt obligation. Such securities are short term (usually called treasury bills, with original maturities of less than one year) or long term (usually called Government bonds or dated securities with original maturity of one year or more).

- **Foreign Portfolio Investment (FPI):**

  Foreign portfolio investment (FPI) consists of securities and other financial assets held by investors in another country. It does not provide the investor with direct ownership of a company's assets and is relatively liquid depending on the volatility of the market.

- **India Volatility Index (VIX):**

  India Volatility index measures the amount of volatility that traders expect over the next thirty days in the NSE index. Simply, it is a calculation of price swings investors expect in the market over important market news.

Production Linked Incentive (PLI) Schemes:

Production Linked Incentive, or PLI, scheme of the Government of India is a form of performance-linked incentive to give companies incentives on incremental sales from products manufactured in domestic units. It is aimed at boosting the manufacturing sector and to reduce imports.

Industrial Production (IIP):

The Index of Industrial Production is an index for India which details out the growth of various sectors in an economy such as mineral mining, electricity and manufacturing.

Balance of Payment:

Balance of Payments (BoP) is a systematic record of a country's economic transactions with the rest of the world over a specific period. It includes trade in goods and services, financial transactions, and monetary transfers.

Current Account:

Current Account is a component of the balance of payments that records a country's transactions in goods and services, income, and current transfers with the rest of the world over a specific period. It includes exports and imports, income from investments, and transfers such as foreign aid.

- **A surplus** in the current account signifies more inflows than outflows.
- **A deficit** indicates the opposite, providing insights into a nation's economic interactions with other countries.

Capital Account:

Capital Account is a segment of the balance of payments tracking a country's financial transactions with the rest of the world. It includes the purchase and sale of assets like foreign investments, loans, and capital transfers. A capital account surplus occurs when a country receives more capital inflows than outflows, while a deficit indicates the opposite.

- **External Debt:**

External Debt refers to the total amount a country owes to foreign creditors. It encompasses both public and private sector obligations, including loans, bonds, and other liabilities.

- **Foreign Direct Investment:**

Foreign Direct Investment (FDI) is the investment made by a company or individual from one country into business interests in another country. It involves acquiring a substantial ownership stake, typically at least 10%, in a foreign enterprise.

- **Foreign Institutional Investment:**

Foreign Institutional Investment (FII) involves the investment of funds by foreign institutions, such as mutual funds and hedge funds, into the financial markets of another country. FIIs buy and sell securities, including stocks and bonds, to benefit from market opportunities.

- **Merchandise Imports:**

Merchandise Imports refer to the goods and physical products a country purchases from foreign sources. These imports contribute to a nation's supply chain, meeting domestic demand for various commodities and finished goods.

- **Foreign Exchange Reserve:**

Foreign Exchange Reserves (Forex Reserves) are a country's holdings of foreign currencies and other assets denominated in foreign currencies. These reserves provide stability to the national currency and facilitate international trade. Governments maintain forex reserves to manage exchange rates, ensure liquidity during economic uncertainties, and meet external payment obligations.

- **Gig Economy:**

The Gig Economy is a labour market characterized by short-term, flexible jobs and freelance work, often facilitated by digital platforms. Workers in the gig economy, known as gig workers or freelancers, engage in temporary or project-based work.

- **Nominal GDP Growth:**

Nominal gross domestic product (GDP) is GDP given in current prices, without adjustment for inflation.

- **Recapitalisation:**

It is a type of a corporate restructuring that aims to change a company's capital structure.

- **Dividend Distribution Tax:**

It is the tax imposed by the Government on domestic companies which pay dividends to their investors.

- **Economic Offences:**

Economic offences covers a wide range of offences such as counterfeiting of currency, financial scams, fraud, money laundering, etc.

- **Economic Resilience:**

Economic resilience aims to better prepare regions to anticipate, withstand, and bounce back from any type of shock, disruption, or stress it may experience.

- **Fintech:**

Fintech refers to the integration of technology into offerings by financial services companies to improve their use and delivery to consumers.

- **Non-performing Assets:**

  A Non-performing Asset (NPA) is a loan or advance for which the principal or interest payment remained overdue for a period of 90 days.

- **Liquidity Adjustment Facility (LAF):**

  LAF is a way for banks and financial institutions to raise funds to meet capital requirements. In India, there are two such facilities:

  - MSF: Marginal Standing Facilty
  - SDF: Standard Deposit Facilty

- **Global Economic Shocks:**

  Global economic shocks refer to severe disruptions or unexpected events that significantly impact the entire global economy. Examples include the COVID-19 pandemic, geopolitical conflicts, natural disasters, and abrupt policy changes. These shocks have widespread effects on various economic indicators such as GDP growth, trade, and financial markets.

- **Emergency Credit Linked Guarantee Scheme (ECLGS):**

  ECLGS is a government initiative aimed at providing credit support to businesses, especially MSMEs, during challenging economic conditions. It involves providing guarantees to banks for loans extended to eligible businesses, ensuring increased access to credit.

- **Credit Growth:**

  Credit growth is the expansion of credit in the financial system, measured by changes in the volume of loans extended by banks and other financial institutions. Healthy credit growth supports economic activities, including consumption, investment, and business operations.

- **Revenue Receipts:**

  These are those receipts which neither create any liability nor cause any reduction in the assets of the government.

- **Capital Receipts:**

  These are receipts that create liabilities or reduce financial assets.

- **Non-debt Capital Receipts:**

  Non-debt capital receipts are those which do not incur any future repayment burden for the government.

- **Non-Tax Revenue:**

  Non-Tax revenue comprises mainly of interest receipts on loans to States and Union Territories, dividends and profits from Public Sector Enterprises including surplus of Reserve Bank of India (RBI) transferred to Government of India, receipts from services provided by the Central Government and external grants.

- **Primary Agricultural Credit Society:**

  It is a basic unit and smallest co-operative credit institutions in India. It is a village-level institution that works directly with rural residents. It encourages agriculturists to save, accepts deposits from them, makes loans to deserving borrowers, and collects repayments.

- **MSME (Micro, Small, and Medium Enterprise):**

  The term was introduced by the Government of India in agreement with the Micro, Small & Medium Enterprises Development (MSMED) Act, 2006. MSME is initiated and managed under the Ministry of MSME (MoMSME) are entities engaged in the production, manufacturing, processing, or preservation of goods and commodities.

*****

1.

INDIAN ECONOMY: PAST, PRESENT & FUTURE

INTRODUCTION

Over the course of the last decade, India has showcased a robust and resilient growth story driven by perseverance, ingenuity, and vision. In the face of unprecedented challenges such as the Covid pandemic and geopolitical conflicts, the Indian economy has demonstrated a remarkable ability to bounce back and convert challenges into opportunities while striving to achieve strong, sustainable, balanced, and inclusive growth.

Objective: The chapter takes a look at the Indian growth experience since independence, the state of the economy, the key drivers of growth of the present decade, and the outlook till 2030.

THE INDIAN GROWTH STORY (1950 TO 2014)

- **Economic shock after Independence (1950s):** By the time India became independent, her share of world income had shrunk from **22.6 per cent** in 1700 to **3.8 per cent** in 1952. To enable the economy to emerge from the shackles of the colonial regime as well as set itself on the path of growth and modernisation, the government in the 1950s adopted a strategy aimed at achieving economic sufficiency.

- **Outcome:** The decadal average growth rate for this period (1952-60) was 3.9 per cent.

- **War period (1960s):** The 1960s witnessed the Indian economy going through several doldrums (**1962 Sino-Indian war** and the **1965-66 India-Pakistan war**, severe drought in 1965). High rates of taxation and pervasive control of the economy also played a key role.

> **Economic growth slowed down** in all parts of the world during the second half of the 1970s and the first half of the 1980s. This slowdown was reversed during the 1980s, primarily driven by the initiation of some reform measures aimed at increasing domestic competitiveness, including the removal of price controls, initiation of fiscal reforms, a revamp of the public sector, reductions in import duties, and de-licensing of the domestic industry.

- **Outcome:** It led to slowing down of economy and posting a decadal growth rate of 4.1 per cent in the 1960s.

- **Devaluation (1970s):** The 1970s witnessed a devaluation of the Indian rupee by a sharp 57 per cent. The decade also witnessed Emergency (1975), Oil shock.
  - **Outcome:** A sharp downfall in the decadal average growth rate in the 1970s to 2.9 per cent.

The devaluation of Indian currency has positive and negative impact on Indian economy. Devaluation means officially lowering the value of currency in terms of foreign exchange.

NEGATIVE IMPACT	POSITIVE IMPACT
■ Increased import cost ■ Increased cost of overseas borrowing ■ Raises inflation ■ Raises the cost of imports and increases demand for indigenous goods ■ It makes imported raw materials more expensive for Indian industries, which increases their cost of production.	■ Economy becomes more attractive to foreign buyers ■ Reduces imports by making exports more affordable for home customers than imports ■ Reduces the current account deficit. ■ Increase in tourism

- **Reform period (1980s): Economic growth slowed down** in all parts of the world during the second half of the 1970s and the first half of the 1980s. This slowdown was reversed during the 1980s, due to reform measures including the removal of price controls, initiation of fiscal reforms, a revamp of the public sector, reductions in import duties, and de-licensing of the domestic industry.
    - **Outcome:** It led to GDP growth improving to 5.7 per cent in the 1980s.
- **Balance-of-Payments (BoP) crisis (1990s):** The external shock (breakup of the **Soviet Bloc** and the Iraq-Kuwait war) adversely contributed to the trade and disrupted the current account balances during 1990-1991.
    - **Outcome:** It led to the balance of payment crisis. All in all, the real GDP growth averaged 5.8 per cent per annum in the 1990s.

Effects of current account deficit for an economy:

- Dependence on foreign borrowing
- A decline in international reserves
- Devaluation of the currency, as it increases the demand for foreign currency and decreases the demand for the country's own currency.
- Increased inflation
- Reduced economic growth

- **Sustained momentum in domestic economic activity (early 2000s):** The growth dividends from the transformative reforms undertaken during the period 1998-2002 played a key role in this regard. There was a global growth boom, and capital flows to India boomed. Measures such as **Sarva Shiksha Abhiyan (SSA), National Rural Health Mission (NRHM), and National Rural Employment Guarantee Scheme (NREGS),** among others.
    - **Outcome:** India's decadal average growth rate in the 2000s was 6.3 per cent per annum.
    - **Global financial crisis (2008):** It exposed the fragile foundations of the growth spurt, and the edifice cracked. Bad debts in banks

began to pile up. The bad debt ratio was soon to hit double-digit percentages. It crested at 11.2 per cent in the year ending March 2018. Much of the bad debt originated between 2006 and 2008.

- **Sustainment of high growth (2009-2014):** India experienced annual **double-digit inflation rates** for five years from 2009 to 2014. The country had to contend with **high twin deficits – both fiscal deficit** (4.9 per cent in FY13) and **current account deficit** (4.8 per cent in FY13) and the rupee was overvalued. It all came to a head in 2013 and the Indian rupee crashed against the US dollar. Between 2009 and 2014, the Indian rupee depreciated annually by 5.9 per cent.

LESSONS FROM THE GROWTH EXPERIENCE TILL 2014

- **Transition from a closed economy to an open economy:**
  - The post-1980 period featured several pro-business reforms amid the realisation that the controlled regime was not delivering the expected results. These policy changes included **import liberalisation, export incentives, exchange rate policies, and expansionary fiscal policy**.
  - The **BoP crisis** of 1990-91 triggered a complete overhauling of economic policies to a market economy. Significant trade policy reforms along with revamping of industrial policies, including the withdrawal of industrial licensing and liberalisation of foreign direct investment (FDI), were introduced.
- **Transition from the dominance of public investment to public and private investment:** India's private sector became the major engine of growth and employment generation during the 1990s and 2000s.
- **Technology, a key growth driver:** Since the 1980s, India has been slowly and steadily using technology to transform its economy.

> As noted by eminent Indian scientist **Shri. R.A Mashelkar**, "It was through the path of 'techno nationalism' that India developed self-reliance through its technologies in both civilian sectors as well as strategic sectors such as space, defence, nuclear energy, and supercomputers".

2014-2024: DECADE OF TRANSFORMATIVE GROWTH

The Indian economy has undergone many structural reforms that have strengthened its macroeconomic fundamentals. These reforms have led to India emerging as the fastest-growing economy among G20 economies.

- **Growth rate:** In 2023-24, as per current estimates, it is estimated to have grown 7.3 per cent on top of the 9.1 per cent (FY22) and 7.2 per cent (FY23) in the previous two years, and the economy is generating jobs.
  - This impressive post-pandemic recovery has seen the urban unemployment rate decline to 6.6 per cent.
- **Social security:** Since May 2023, the number of net new subscribers to EPFO in the age group 18-25 years has consistently exceeded 55 per cent of the total net new EPF subscribers.
  - The government has extended the **Pradhan Mantri Gharib Kalyan Anna Yojana** for 80 crore citizens for five more years until December 2028.
- **Infrastructure:** The government is building a **road network and expanding rail and air networks** at a record pace.

> - **Road network:** India boasts of the world's second-largest road network, with over 6.37 million kilometres.
> - **Railways**: India's railways have undergone substantial modernization and expansion. Capital expenditure on railway infrastructure has steadily increased over the past four years, with a budget of ₹2.5 lakh crore allocated in FY22-23, representing a 29% rise compared to the previous year.
> - **Ports**: There are 12 major ports and over 200 non-major ports in the country, along the 7,500-km long coastline.
> - **Airports:** As many as 131 airports are in operation in India.

- **Education:** The number of universities was 723 in 2014, and it increased to 1,113 in 2023.
  - More girls are now in higher education than boys. The Gross Enrolment Ratio (GER) for girls is 27.9 in 2020 vis-à-vis 12.7 per cent in FY10.

- Total enrolment in higher education was 3.4 crore in 2014. It has gone up to 4.1 crore students in 2023.

- **Oil:** Further, the government, despite the conflict in Ukraine and disrupted supplies, has managed crude oil purchases at the right price so that retail prices of petrol and diesel did not have to be increased for more than eighteen months.
- **State infrastructure**: The government gave a 50-year interest free loan of ₹1 lakh crore to states in FY23 and announced another ₹1.3 lakh crore of 50-year interest-free loan in FY24.
    - Resultingly, the states are improving their infrastructure, like **schools, rural roads, electricity provision, etc.**

DRIVERS OF INDIA'S GROWTH IN THE LAST DECADE

- **Strong financial sector:** As the banking, non-banking, and nonfinancial sectors de-leveraged their balance sheets, the government undertook several reforms to strengthen the financial sector:
    - Recapitalisation and merger of **Public Sector Banks (PSB)**
    - Amendment of the SARFAESI Act 2002
    - Enacting the Insolvency and Bankruptcy Code 2016 (IBC)
    - Simplification of regulatory frameworks
- **Effective taxation system:** To enhance the ease of living and ease of doing business, the taxation ecosystem in the country has undergone substantial changes such as:
    - adopting a unified Goods and Services Tax (GST)
    - reducing corporate and income tax rates
    - exemption of sovereign wealth funds and pension funds from taxes
    - removing the Dividend Distribution tax
    - The GST system has shown improved buoyancy over the pre-GST regime with consistently rising average monthly gross collections from ₹0.9 lakh crore in FY18 to ₹1.5 lakh crore in FY23.

GST

- GST was introduced through the 101st Constitution Amendment Act, 2016.
- It is one of the biggest indirect tax reforms in the country.
- It was introduced with the slogan of 'One Nation One Tax'.

Significance of GST	Issues associated with GST
■ Create a Unified Common Market ■ Streamline Taxation ■ Increase Tax Compliance ■ Discourage Tax evasion ■ Reduce Corruption ■ Boost Secondary Sector	■ While GST scrapped multiplicity of taxes and cesses, a new levy in the form of compensation cess was introduced for luxury, sin or demerit goods. This was later expanded to include automobiles. ■ Economy outside GST purview: Nearly half the economy remains outside GST. E.g. petroleum, real estate, electricity duties remain outside GST purview. ■ Higher Tax Rates: Though rates are rationalised, there is still 50% of items are under the 18% bracket.

- **Private sector:** The private sector is now entrusted as a **co-partner** in development.
  - **A New Public Sector Enterprise (PSE) Policy for Aatmanirbhar Bharat** has been introduced to minimise the presence of the government in the PSEs to only a few strategic sectors.
  - Initiatives are introduced under **Aatmanirbhar Bharat and Make in India Programmes.**
  - **Production Linked Incentives (PLI)** are being provided to firms to attract domestic and foreign investments and to develop global champions in the manufacturing industry.
  - Strategic sectors, such as **defence, mining, and space,** have been opened up to enhance business opportunities for the private sector.

- **The FDI policy** has also been further liberalised, with most sectors now open for 100 per cent FDI under the automatic route.
    - **Decriminalising minor economic offences** under the Companies Act of 2013 has significantly enhanced the ease of doing business over the past years.

- **MSMEs:** The progressive reforms introduced for the **Micro, Small, and Medium Enterprises (MSME)** sector have supported smaller businesses to recover from the impact of the pandemic and grow further. Some of these are:
    - Emergency Credit Line Guarantee Scheme (ECLGS)

> **Emergency Credit Line Guarantee Scheme (ECLGS)** was launched in 2020 as part of Aatmanirbhar Bharat Abhiyan to **support eligible MSMEs** and business enterprises in meeting their operational liabilities and restarting their businesses in the context of the disruption caused by the COVID-19 pandemic.

- Revision in the definition of MSMEs under the ambit of Aatmanirbhar Bharat
- Introduction of TReDS

> **Trade Receivables electronic Discounting System (TReDS)** is an online electronic platform and an institutional mechanism for factoring of trade receivables of MSME sellers. It enables discounting of invoices through an auction mechanism to ensure prompt realisation of trade receivables.

- Inclusion of retail and wholesale trades as MSMEs
    - The number of recognised start-ups has increased from 452 in 2016 to more than 98,000 in 2023.

> **What is MSME?**
> MSMEs are micro, small, and medium enterprises that engage in the service sector or the manufacturing, processing, production, and preservation of goods.

CLASSIFICATION	MICRO	SMALL	MEDIUM
Manufacturing Enterprises and Enterprises rendering Services **(Investment in Plant and Machinery or Equipment)**	Not more than ₹1 crore and Annual Turnover: not more than ₹5 crore	Not more than ₹10 crore and Annual Turnover: not more than ₹50 crore	Not more than ₹50 crore and Annual Turnover: not more than ₹250 crore

National Logistics Policy 2022 seeks to address challenges facing the transport sector and bring down the logistics cost for businesses from 13-14% to a single digit. The policy was announced for the first time in the Union Budget 2020.

- **Infrastructure:** The effective Capital Expenditure has risen from 2.8 per cent of GDP in the fiscal year ending March 2014 to 4.5 per cent in 2023-24 (BE). Dedicated programs for road connectivity **(Bharatmala)**, port infrastructure **(Sagarmala)**, electrification, railways upgradation, and new airports/air routes **(UDAN)** have enabled the modernisation of infrastructure. An overarching logistics ecosystem supports this enabling infrastructure through the **National Logistics Policy 2022.**
- Inclusive growth policies:
  - Over 10.11 crore women have been given free gas connections
  - 11.72 crore toilets have been built for the poor
  - 51.6 crore **Jan Dhan accounts** have been opened
  - 3.24 beneficiaries have been registered
  - 2.6 crore pucca houses have been built for the poor people
  - 6.27 crore hospital admissions have been done under the **Ayushman Bharat Scheme**

- **Prime Minister's Jan Dhan Yojana (PMJDY): This** initiative is aimed at universal banking access by providing zero-balance bank accounts to unbanked households. It has helped bring over 50 crore people into the formal banking system.

WHAT ARE THE CHALLENGES CONFRONTING THE INDIAN ECONOMY?

- **Increased geo-economic fragmentation and the slowdown of hyper-globalisation** are likely to result in further friend shoring and onshoring, which are already having repercussions on global trade and, subsequently, on global growth.
- **Trade-off between energy security and economic growth versus energy transition** is a multifaceted issue having various dimensions: geopolitical, technological, fiscal, economic and social, and the policy actions being pursued by individual countries impacting other economies.

> In an **IMF paper**, it has been estimated that **40 per cent of global employment is exposed to AI**, with the benefits of complementarity operating beside the risks of displacement.

- **Advent of Artificial Intelligence (AI)** poses a big challenge to governments around the world due to the questions it poses to employment particularly in services sectors.
- **Skilled Workforce:** Domestically, ensuring the availability of a talented and appropriately skilled workforce to the industry, age-appropriate learning outcomes in schools at all levels and a healthy and fit population are important policy priorities in the coming years.

Important progress recorded:

- **Pradhan Mantri Kaushal Vikas Yojana (PMKVY)** aims to enable Indian youth to take up relevant industry skill training that will help them secure a better livelihood. As of December 2023, around 1.3 crore candidates have received training under PMKVY.
- **Aadhar** has been a major game changer across domains in India. It has facilitated the transfer of over 34 lakh crores to more than 1167 crore beneficiaries under the Direct Benefit Transfer, and on average, more than 200 crore Aadhaar-based authentications are happening every month.

- **Total beneficiaries under the Prime Minister's Jan Dhan Yojana** were at 51.5 crore as of January 10, 2024, which has grown three-fold (3.5) since March 2015.
- With the **CoWin app**, India has been successful in implementing one of the world's largest vaccination programs, with 221 crore vaccination doses administered to the population aged 18 years and above.
- **Satellites:** Up to July 2023, India had launched 431 foreign satellites, out of which 396 had been launched since June 2014.
- **Internet penetration** in India, as per the 'Internet in India' report 2022, crossed the 50 per cent mark in 2022, growing more than three-fold since 2014.

LOOKING AHEAD

By all estimates, India's growth is expected to remain strong, supported by macroeconomic and financial stability. Presently, the official estimate for growth in FY24 stands at 7.3 per cent and the headline inflation is expected to gradually decline to the target. India embarks on her 'Amrit Kaal' with confidence and the attitude that challenges to growth and inclusive development are stepping stones and not obstacles.

Important Schemes

- **Bharatmala Pariyojana:** Launched in 2017, it is a government-funded mega roads and highways project in India, under which the Central government plans to build a robust high-speed road network across the country.
- **Sagarmala** is a National Perspective Plan (NPP) for the comprehensive development of India's 7,500 km coastline, 14,500 km of potentially navigable waterways and maritime sector. The Sagarmala concept was approved in 2015.
- **UDAN:** The **Regional Connectivity Scheme (RCS)-Ude Desh ka Aam Nagrik (UDAN) infrastructure scheme** was initiated in October 2016 with the objective of fulfilling the aspirations of the common citizen, with an enhanced aviation infrastructure and air connectivity in tier II and tier III cities.

*****

2.

WHAT MADE THE INDIAN ECONOMY RESILIENT?

INTRODUCTION

Objective: The chapter focuses on the measures that the government has taken in the past 10 years in several aspects of public policy, which have contributed to the post-Covid economic resilience and set India on a path to sustained economic growth in the coming years. More specifically, these have been identified across four blocks in this chapter:

- Domestic Economy
- Macroeconomic Stability
- Human Resources
- External Economy

DOMESTIC ECONOMY

India's real GDP is estimated to grow at an average of 7.9 per cent between FY22 and FY24. The contribution to growth is due, in no small measure, to those sectors in which the government has taken specific measures.

- **Share of manufacturing**: The share of manufacturing in total Gross Value Added (GVA), in volume terms, increased from 17.2 per cent in FY14 to 18.4 per cent in FY18 under the impact of the Make in India mission of the government.

- **Measures:** Production Linked Incentive (PLI) schemes.

- **Share of construction**: After countering a sharp increase in the prices of real estate and the pandemic, the share has almost recovered to reach 8.7 per cent in FY24.
  - **Measures**: A slight moderation in prices and wealth effect from the accumulated financial assets of the households, setting up of the **Real Estate Regulatory Authority (RERA)**, significant upscaling of government capex.
- **Share of services**: The share of services in total GVA, in volume terms, has risen from 51.1 per cent in FY14 to 54.6 per cent in FY24, as the pandemic and unlocking of the economy thereafter led to a surge in non-contact services.
  - **Measures:** IBC and government capex push, has strengthened consumption and investment.

Resilience of consumption demand

- **Private Final Consumption Expenditure (PFCE)** has consequently emerged as a major growth driver post-Covid pandemic. The share of PFCE in GDP at current prices increased from an average of 58.4 per cent in the eight years preceding the onset of the pandemic to 60.8 per cent in the last three years ending FY24 (Figure 1).

FIGURE 1: Share of Private Final Consumption Expenditure in GDP

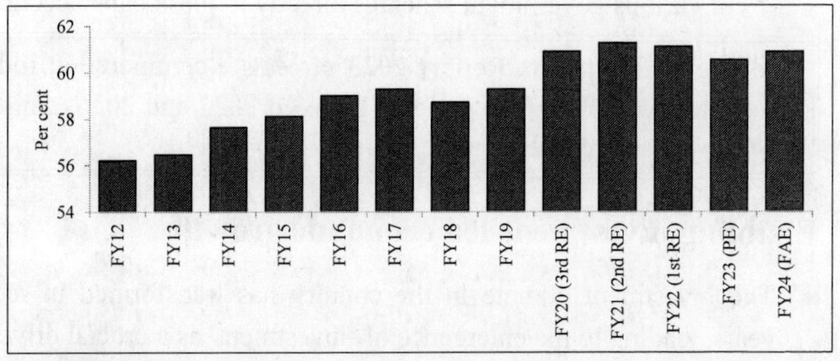

Source: NSO, MoSPI

Note: RE stands for Revised Estimates, PE for Provisional Estimates and FAE for First Advance Estimates

- **Per Capita Real Gross National Income (GNI):** The secured consumption base resulted from the robust increase in Per Capita Real Gross National Income (GNI) that registered a compounded annual growth rate (CAGR) of 5.3 per cent from FY12 to FY20.
- **Public digital infrastructure:** Besides the structural reforms, the government's emphasis on developing public digital infrastructure has also been a game changer.

> **Chapter 3 of Economic Survey 2022-23** discussed in detail the gains from digitalisation through enhanced financial inclusion, formalisation of the economy, efficient service delivery and transparent governance processes.

  - **Aarogya Setu and CoWin apps** proved to be game changers, helping to track and contain the spread of the virus and facilitating the vaccination of many people in a short period.
  - During the pandemic, when mobility was restricted, there was a pronounced shift in **virtual healthcare visits**, digital payments, and the acceleration of **e-grocery shopping**.
  - **Digital payment systems** like **Unified Payments Interface (UPI),** which has one of the largest platforms in the world, have aided the growth of e-commerce.
  - **Pradhan Mantri Jan Dhan Yojana (PMJDY)** provided access to low-cost bank accounts to a large unbanked population, and **Direct Benefit Transfer (DBT)** eased the transferring of benefits of various government schemes directly to these bank accounts.

> The **Global Payments Report 2023** projects e-commerce in India to register a CAGR of 16 per cent between 2022 and 2026, mainly driven by ease provided by UPI.

Enabling investment-led economic growth

- The investment climate in the country has transformed in recent years, leading to the emergence of 'investment' as a crucial driver of economic growth.

- The government helped banks strengthen their balance sheets by recapitalising them and restructuring the industry. With stronger balance sheets in the non-financial corporate and banking sectors, growth in investments and credit are poised to increase in this decade, as is already evident in the data for the last three years (Figure 2).

FIGURE 2: Trends in Investment Rate Over the Years

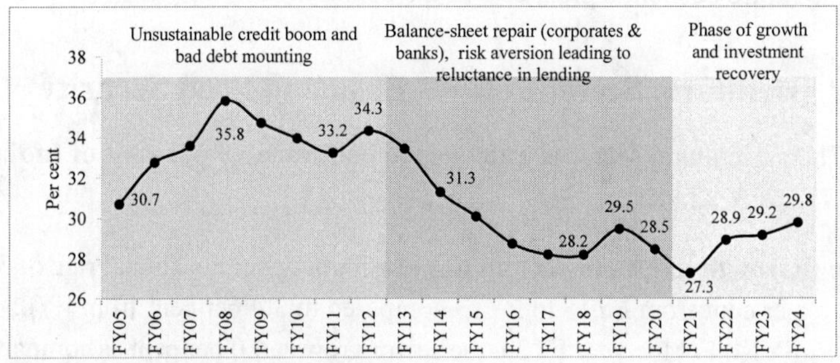

Note: Investment Rate is the ratio of Nominal GFCF
Data for FY24 is as per the First Advance Estimates
Source: NSO

- Alongside, the government also sped up work on the **large pipeline of infrastructure projects** that had stalled due to construction delays, inefficient administrative processes, inadequate financing, and legal and land issues.
- **Digitalising bureaucratic procedures**, streamlining approvals of investment projects, easing legal constraints, creating a supportive tax eco-system with reduced corporate tax rates and a uniform GST regime, and opening new avenues for private investors have ensured a non-adversarial policy environment.
  - For instance, the **Pragati/Project Monitoring Group (PMG) mechanism** has been a game-changer in expediting the execution of long-delayed projects. Since June 2014, 2,169 projects worth ₹49.4 lakh crore have been on-boarded on the PMG portal.
- **Index of Industrial Production (IIP)** data shows that the **capital goods index** and infrastructure/construction goods index saw robust growth of 12.9 per cent and 8.4 per cent, respectively, in FY23.

- **Rising household investments in real estate**: The household sector investment, which constitutes the largest share in the total Gross Fixed Capital Formation. The average annual growth in real-estate prices has increased from 2.3 per cent in FY22 to 3.8 per cent in FY23 and 4.3 per cent in H1 of FY24.

The increase in investments is driven by all three sectors of the economy - **public sector, private sector, and households**, reflecting confidence in the future economic prospects of the country.

Agricultural Sector Policies Ensuring Food Security

The agricultural sector is estimated to constitute **18 per cent of India's GVA in FY24**.

- **Growth data:** The sector grew at a higher average annual rate of 3.7 per cent from FY15 to FY23 compared to 3.4 per cent from FY05 to FY14. For the year FY23, the sector grew at 4.0 per cent as compared to the previous year.
- **Grain production:** The total food grains production for FY23 was 329.7 million tonnes, marking a rise of 14.1 million tonnes compared to the previous year.
    - **Rice, wheat, pulses, Nutri/coarse cereals, and oilseeds** witnessed record increases in production.
    - India's global dominance extends across agricultural commodities, making it the largest producer of **milk, pulses, and spices** worldwide.
    - Additionally, India ranks second-largest producer of **fruits, vegetables, tea, farmed fish, sugarcane, wheat, rice, cotton, and sugar.**
- **Agriculture export:** The improved performance is also reflected in a substantial surge in agriculture exports, reaching ₹4.2 lakh crore in FY23.
- **Government's strategic measures:** consistent increase in **Minimum Support Prices (MSPs)** for 22 **Kharif** and **Rabi crops, Pradhan Mantri Kisan Maandhan Yojana (PM-KMY), Pradhan Mantri**

Kisan Samman Nidhi (PM-KISAN), and **Pradhan Mantri Fasal Bima Yojana (PMFBY).**

- To ensure remunerative prices to the farmers for their produce, the government introduced the **Pradhan Mantri Annadata Aay Sanrakshan Abhiyan (PM-AASHA)** scheme in 2018.

> - PM-KISAN, launched in 2019, supplements the financial needs of landholding farmers by transferring ₹6,000 per year in three equal four-monthly instalments.

- **Digital inclusion:** The launch of digital platform **e-NAM (National Agriculture Market)** in 2016 has facilitated the integration of **Agriculture Produce Marketing Committees (APMC) mandis** and has provided multi-faceted.
  - The number of markets linked to the e-NAM platform has increased from 250 in 2016 to 1,389 in 2023.
- **Strengthening the cooperative movement:** The government computerised **Primary Agricultural Credit Societies (PACS).** The government has also created **Agristack**, a federated architecture for effective planning, monitoring, policy-making, strategy formulation, and implementation of schemes.
- **Enhancement in post-harvest infrastructure investment: Agriculture Infrastructure Fund (AIF)** and **Pradhan Mantri Kisan Sampada Yojana (PMKSY),** adoption of sustainable agriculture practices like the **Per Drop More Crop** Component of the **Pradhan Mantri Krishi Sinchayi Yojana (PMKSY-PDMC)** and promotion of Natural Farming to transform agriculture making it more resilient.
- **Challenges:** global health crisis and variability in climate conditions.

Agriculture

Current Status of Agriculture

- **Growth Rate:** In 2020-21, the growth in this sector was 3.3%. In 2016-17, the growth rate was 6.8%, followed by 6.6% in 2017-18, 2.1% in 2018-19 and 5.5% in 2019-20.

- **Investment:** Private investment in agriculture increased to 9.3% in 2020-21. The public investment, however, remained at 4.3%, the same as 2019-20.
  - In 2011-12, the public investment in agriculture was 5.4%.
- **Export:** During 2021-22, agricultural exports reached an all-time high of US$ 50.2 billion.
- **Employment generation**: In terms of employment, the agriculture sector provides livelihood to over 151 million people. Approximately 60 per cent of the Indian population works in the industry.
- **Contribution in GDP:** The sector is contributing about 18 per cent to India's GDP.
  - This share decreases gradually with each year, with development in other areas of the country's economy.
- Agriculture and allied sectors which include forestry and fisheries contribute to over 24 per cent to the country's GVA (gross value added).

Major constraints in Indian agriculture	Suggestive measures
■ Low access of credit ■ Low Credit supply ■ Low penetration of Technology ■ Less Value-addition at primary level ■ Poor Irrigation Infrastructure ■ Exhaustion of soils ■ Improper Supply Chain Management ■ Inadequate storage facilities	■ Automation in Agriculture: ■ Improved Storage and Supply-Chain Facilities ■ Application of Nano-Technology ■ Application of Biotechnology ■ Digital Agriculture ■ Cost-effective technologies ■ The sector needs to engage with fair and responsible production and trade issues on a priority basis even for domestic markets. ■ Protective measures for small producers

■ There is more dependence on weather, marketing and supply chain suitable for high value crops. ■ **Small land holding:** According to 2010-11 Agriculture Census, the total number of operational holdings was 138.35 million with average size of 1.15 hectares (ha). ➤ Of the total holdings, 85 per cent are in marginal and small farm categories of less than 2 ha (GOI, 2014).	■ Institutional innovation ■ Crop diversification

Reform push to the Indian Industry

- **Growth rate:** Industrial growth accelerated to 7.1 per cent per annum from FY15 to FY19, compared to 5.5 per cent in the preceding five-year block of FY10 to FY14. The Indian Industry is likely to record a robust 8 per cent growth per annum during the triennium ending March 2024, as indicated by the first advance estimates of National Accounts for FY24.

Strategic Initiatives Undertaken by the Government

- **Make in India initiative:** The government took targeted measures under the 'Make in India' initiative to bolster domestic manufacturing and promote self-reliance across various industries.
- **PLI scheme:** The PLI scheme covers 14 sectors, designed to incentivise manufacturers to increase production and exports.

How PLI Scheme is a game-changer for the economy?

- Production Linked Incentive scheme (PLI) has become a crucial part of the vision of making India a $ 5 trillion economy. In the post-pandemic scenario, PLI is proving to be a huge catalyst in creating 'Aatmanirbhar Bharat'.
- The scheme currently targets 14 sectors of strategic and economic importance for India's economic growth.
- The 14 sectors are: **(i) Mobile Manufacturing and Specified Electronic Components, (ii) Critical Key Starting Materials/ Drug Intermediaries & Active Pharmaceutical Ingredients, (iii) Manufacturing of Medical Devices (iv) Automobiles and Auto Components, (v) Pharmaceuticals Drugs, (vi) Specialty Steel, (vii) Telecom & Networking Products, (viii) Electronic/ Technology Products, (ix) White Goods (ACs and LEDs), (x) Food Products, (xi) Textile Products: MMF segment and technical textiles, (xii) High efficiency solar PV modules, (xiii) Advanced Chemistry Cell (ACC) Battery, and (xiv) Drones and Drone Components.**
- The purpose of the PLI Schemes is to
  - attract investments in key sectors and cutting-edge technology
  - ensure efficiency and bring economies of size and scale in the manufacturing sector
  - make Indian companies and manufacturers globally competitive
- These schemes have the potential of significantly boosting production, employment and economic growth over the next five years or so.

- **Start-up India Initiative**: The 1.14 lakh start-ups (as of October 2023) recognised by the government under the Start-up India Initiative have reported the creation of more than 12 lakh jobs.
- **Open Network for Digital Commerce** has recorded more than 6.3 million transactions in November 2023.
- **Regulatory reforms**: Decriminalisation of 3,600 compliances, have improved the ease of doing business.

- The Jan Vishwas Amendment Bill 2023, passed by the Parliament, proposes to decriminalise 183 provisions across 42 Central Acts administered by 19 Ministries/Departments.

■ **MSMEs** are becoming increasingly vibrant and dynamic. The **Udyam portal** and the **Udyam Assist Platform (UAP)** have helped consolidate the information on MSMEs, with 2.24 crore MSMEs registered on the Udyam portal and about 1.2 crore units registered on the UAP.

- The **PM Vishwakarma**, introduced in 2023, offering holistic end-to-end support to the artisans and craftspeople, has already attracted 48.8 lakh enrolments as of the end of December 2023.
- Under the **Pradhan Mantri Mudra Yojana**, loans amounting to ₹25.98 lakh crore have so far been disbursed to non-corporate, non-farm small and micro enterprises.
- The limit of credit guarantee under the **Credit Guarantee Fund Trust for Micro & Small Enterprises (CGTMSE)** was raised from ₹2 crore to ₹5 crore in April 2023, and its corpus increased to enable additional credit.
- Under the **Emergency Credit Line Guarantee Scheme (ECLGS),** announced under the Aatmanirbhar Bharat package, guarantees to the tune of ₹2.4 lakh crore have been provided.

Digital Infrastructure and Delivery of Citizen-Centric Services

■ India's world-class **digital public infrastructure (DPI),** also referred to as **India Stack**, has enabled online, paperless, and cashless digital access to various public and private services. The India Stack consists of three interconnected layers:

- **The Identity Layer (Aadhaar):** providing a digital identity to every Indian.
- **The Payments Layer (Unified Payments Interface, Aadhaar Payments Bridge, Aadhaar Enabled Payment Service):** enabling surge of cashless payments.

- **The Data Layer (Account Aggregator):** transforming the authentication ecosystem in India and facilitated the KYC process.

- **PMJDY:** Launched in 2014, it put to great use the Indian Stack to enable direct benefit transfers straight into the bank account of the beneficiary using the Aadhar and the mobile connect.
- **PM eVIDYA** was launched with the use of digital technology to bridge learning gaps during the pandemic.
- The **Digital Document Execution platform** of **National EGovernance Services Limited (NeSL),** an Information Utility set up under the IBC, rapidly completes the loan documentation of a beneficiary.
- India is among the fastest-growing fintech markets in the World, hailing as the **third-largest growing fintech economy** after the USA and the UK.

> As per a report by **UNICOMMERCE on 'India E-Commerce Index 2023',** the overall order volume witnessed a growth of 26.2 per cent in FY23, indicating a flourishing ecommerce landscape in India, supported by a 23.5 per cent rise in annual Gross Merchandise Value (GMV) as compared to FY22.

Credit creation is back

Bank credit, in recent years, has shown phenomenal growth, outpacing the growth in deposits on the back of sustained demand momentum and robust economic recovery after the Covid-19 pandemic. The growth in non-food bank credit at 15 per cent in FY23 was the highest in the last 10 years.

- **RBI's AQR and PCA framework:** The deterioration in the asset quality of Indian banks became visible after the RBI implemented the **'Asset Quality Review' (AQR)** and **prompt corrective action (PCA) framework** in FY15 to increase transparency in the financial sector.

- **IBC:** The government enacted the IBC in 2016, along with the amendment of the Banking Regulation Act of 1949. This facilitated a speedier resolution of bad debt and helped improve the credit repayment culture.
- **Emergency Credit Linked Guarantee Scheme (ECLGS):** While the RBI eased repayment stress, the government launched the Emergency Credit Linked Guarantee Scheme (ECLGS) to extend large volumes of credit to MSMEs. Bank credit to MSMEs registered a Compound Annual Growth Rate (CAGR) of 14.2 per cent from FY19 to FY24 (as of November 17, 2023).
- **NBFC regulations:** A revised scale based regulatory framework has been implemented to harmonise the regulations of NBFCs with those of banks, wherever appropriate. The formal PCA framework was extended to NBFCs to enable supervisory intervention at appropriate times and require the supervised entity to initiate and implement remedial measures in a timely manner to restore its financial health.

Evolving financial markets to support the investment needs of a growing economy

- Indian financial markets have gone from strength to strength over the last decade.
- **India's equity markets** have outperformed major global markets. The Indian benchmark equity indices – the BSE Sensex and the Nifty 50 - delivered a CAGR of about 13.5 per cent in the period January 2014 – December 2023.
- **Volatility** in 2023, as measured by the standard deviation of the weekly returns of the benchmark BSE Sensex, has also come down to levels last observed in 2019.
- **Growth in demat accounts**: The number of demat accounts in India increased to 13.9 crore at the end of December 2023 marking a 536 per cent growth from the total number of accounts as at the end of March 2014.
- **Accelerating activity in the equity markets** has led to companies significantly increasing the number of IPO issuances, particularly in the small and medium enterprises (SME) segment.

- Since FY15, 1,050 companies cumulatively have gone public and raised capital worth ₹3.9 lakh crore, as compared to 441 companies mobilising ₹1.5 lakh crore in the preceding 9 year period.

■ As per SEBI, significant interest from domestic and global investors in the Indian stock market as an attractive investment destination and sustained IPO activity has placed **the Indian market fifth in the world by market capitalisation**.

■ **India's market capitalisation to GDP ratio** has improved significantly over the last nine years, from 79 per cent at the end of 2014 to 104 per cent at the end of 2022, far higher than that of other emerging market economies like China and Brazil.

■ The performance of Indian equity markets has enabled India to secure the **second-largest weightage in the MSCI Emerging Markets index.**

■ **Bonds segment**: In 2023, India's **sovereign bond yields** remained range-bound even as advanced economies experienced a tumultuous year for sovereign bond yields. The credit spread between the US and India sovereign bond yields narrowed to historic lows, reflecting India's robust macroeconomic fundamentals.

Important initiatives:

■ **RBI's Retail Direct scheme** allowed individual investors to subscribe to government securities such as **sovereign bonds and sovereign gold bonds.**

■ **Sovereign green bonds:** RBI introduced the sovereign green bonds, the proceeds of which will be used to fund the construction and operation of green projects.

■ **InvITs and Municipal Bonds**: SEBI introduced regulations for new instruments such as **InvITs and Municipal Bonds** to facilitate more efficient infrastructure financing through the capital markets.

■ **SEBI's framework for corporate bond market:** To provide further impetus to the **corporate bond market**, SEBI introduced a framework whereby listed large corporates will mandatorily meet

25 per cent of their financing needs through the issuance of debt securities.

These measures are expected to yield dividends in the coming decade. There is evidence of robust investor interest in India's bond markets following the decision by **JP Morgan to include India's sovereign bonds** on its widely tracked **Emerging Markets Government Bond Index**.

SAFEGUARDING MACROECONOMIC STABILITY

What is Macroeconomic Stabilization?

- Macroeconomic stabilization is a condition in which a complex framework for monetary and fiscal institutions and policies is established to reduce volatility and encourage welfare-enhancing growth.
- Achieving this condition requires aligning currency to market levels, managing inflation, establishing foreign exchange facilities, developing a national budget, generating revenue, creating a transparent system of public expenditure, and preventing predatory actors from controlling the country's resources

Macroeconomic stability built on an economic environment with strong output growth, price stability, and robust external account are important goals of the government and the Reserve Bank of India.

Inflation

- **Reigning in inflation with flexible targeting:** The period between FY09 and FY14 was marked by high average retail inflation of 10 per cent and high levels of macro-vulnerability. Since the advent of flexible inflation-targeting within the band of 4 +/- 2 per cent under the Monetary Policy Framework Agreement in FY16, retail inflation averaged 4.2 per cent till FY20.

- **The Price Stabilization Fund (PSF)** set up in 2014-15 has been effective in tackling price volatility in important Agri-horticultural commodities.
- **Post-pandemic, FY22** saw a revival of the economy, with growth gaining momentum and inflation coming down. However, by the end of FY22, the global economic environment worsened due to
  - **Escalation of geopolitical conflicts** and accompanying sanctions
  - **Global commodity prices shot up** substantially across the board
  - **The above spurred inflation** globally, which affected India's external account and price situation.
  - **Supply chain pressures**, which were set to ease after the pandemic, were rising again. Elevated edible oil prices due to global supply chain disruptions and higher vegetable prices due to uneven weather conditions led to high food inflation.
- To insulate the domestic economy from the vulnerabilities in existing supplies of crude oil and natural gas and to reduce dependency on OPEC, the government diversified the supply sources over the last few years and ensured the availability of energy supply at reasonable prices.
  - This, in no small measure, contributed to India's growth revival.

Food inflation

Impact of global supply disruptions in India

- **Global supply disruptions** (Covid and then the Russia-Ukraine conflict) resulted in domestic retail edible oil inflation soaring to double digits.
- High global prices, likewise, caused runaway inflation in **cereals, particularly wheat**, from the middle of 2022 – in this case, by making exports attractive and exacerbating domestic shortages.
- The scope for such transmission of global inflation to domestic prices in India is, however, largely limited to the two agri-commodities where the country is significantly import-dependent: **Edible oils and pulses.**

- In most others – from **cereals, sugar, dairy and poultry to fruits and vegetables** – India isn't just self-sufficient, but also an exporter.
- Simply put, food inflation in India is today de-globalised.

- **Persistence food inflation** is a global challenge. In India, the prices of specific food items were pressured by **untimely rains**, leading to crop losses and weather-driven supply chain disruptions.
  - **Anti-inflationary policies:** Timely focus on supply-side initiatives, strengthening buffers of key food items and making periodic open market releases, trade policy measures aimed at improving domestic availability of food, preventing hoarding through imposition and revision of stock limits, and channelling supplies of select food items through designated retail outlets

Supportive monetary policy helped greatly. The RBI increased the **policy repo rate** under the **liquidity adjustment facility** progressively from 4 per cent in April 2022 to 6.5 per cent till February 2023 and kept it unchanged thereafter to ensure that inflation aligns with the target while supporting growth.

HUMAN RESOURCES: DOVETAILING GROWTH WITH CAPACITATING WELFARE: A NEW APPROACH TO WELFARE

Social Security System

The social security system in India includes not just an insurance payment of premiums into government funds (like in China) but also lump sum employer obligations.

India's social security schemes cover the following types of social insurance:

- Employee Provident Fund (EPF);
- Health insurance and medical benefits;
- Disability benefit;
- Maternity benefit; and
- Gratuity.

Over the last decade, the Indian concept of welfare has been significantly transformed into a more **long-term-oriented, efficient, and empowering avatar**. This has lent a capacitating edge to welfare and helped lay a solid foundation for human development in the country.

- **Spending on social services:** The Union government expenditure on social services has increased at a CAGR of 5.9 per cent between FY12 and FY23, while the capital expenditure on social services has grown by 8.1 per cent CAGR over the same period, indicating the creation of societal assets.
- **Programmes for universal access to basic amenities** (such as **Ujjwala Yojana, PM-Jan Aarogya Yojana, PM-Jal Jeevan Mission, and PM-AWAS Yojana**, among others) have gained prominence.
- **Fiscal efficiency:** The **DBT scheme** and **Jan Dhan Yojana-Aadhaar-Mobile (JAM) trinity** have been boosters of fiscal efficiency and minimisation of leakages. More recently, the **'One Nation One Ration Card'** programme, allowing seamless portability of ration cards across states for migrant workers, represents the institutionalisation of digital goods in welfare.

Initiatives

- **Pradhan Mantri Ujjwala Yojana (PMUY):** In 2016, **Ministry of Petroleum and Natural Gas (MOPNG)**, introduced the 'Pradhan Mantri Ujjwala Yojana' (PMUY) as a flagship scheme with an **objective to make clean cooking fuel such as LPG available to the rural and deprived households** which were otherwise using traditional cooking fuels such as firewood, coal, cow-dung cakes etc.
- **Atal Pension Yojana (APY)** aims to create a universal social security system for all Indians, especially the poor, the under-privileged and the workers in the unorganised sector. APY is administered by **Pension Fund Regulatory and Development Authority (PFRDA)** under the overall administrative and institutional architecture of the **National Pension System (NPS).**

- **Pradhan Mantri Jeevan Jyoti Bima Yojana (PMJJBY):** PMJJBY is a one-year life insurance scheme renewable from year to year offering coverage for death due to any reason.
- **Stand-Up India Scheme:** was launched in 2016 to promote entrepreneurship at grassroot level focusing on economic empowerment and job creation. This scheme has been extended up to the year 2025.

- **Affordable social security schemes** (unorganised sector workers): The **Atal Pension Yojana (APY), PM Jeevan Jyoti Yojana (PMJJY), and PM Suraksha Bima Yojana (PMSBY)** (all three launched in 2015) are success stories of an expanding social safety net equipped with universal bank account penetration.
    - While PMJJY and PMSBY were the first of their kind, the APY improved remarkably upon its predecessor, the Swavalamban Yojana.
    - The subscriber base of the Atal Pension Yojana in December 2023 stands at 6.1 crore, 30 times the base of 20.7 lakh in FY15.

The new approach to welfare was also manifested in India's response to the "once in a century" crisis of Covid-19 when the government opted for a phased response coupled with safety nets for vulnerable sections while responding iteratively to the emerging Covid-19 situation rather than emptying its coffers in panic. The calibrated response helped address the specific needs of the sections at risk, ensuring food security, credit for street vendors, employment for returnee migrants, etc., while sectors of the economy recovered at different paces.

New welfare approach

The evolution of the **new welfare approach** has culminated in a large-scale improvement in the **quality of life** in India. With India becoming the 5th largest economy, the lives of the common person look remarkably better than a decade ago.

Significant improvements

- According to a **NITI Aayog report**, 13.5 crore Indians escaped multidimensional poverty between 2015-16 and 2019-21. This trend is driven by rural India and the most backward areas, demonstrating the ideal of "Antyodaya".
- **The National Family Health Survey data** for 2019-21 shows a consistent rise in access to electricity, drinking water, sanitation, clean fuel, etc.
- **National health accounts data** shows a consistent decline in out-of-pocket health expenditure from 62.6 per cent of total health expenditure (THE) in FY15 to 47.1 per cent of THE in FY20.
- There is a decline in the **maternal mortality ratio** from 130 per lakh live births in 2014-16 to 97 per lakh live births in 2018-20.
- The female GER in higher education overtaking the male GER since FY18, etc.

EXPANSION OF THE BIG TENT UNDER THE NEW WELFARE APPROACH

Affordable and Wholesome Health	■ 30.3 crore **Ayushman Bharat cards** created and 6.2 crore hospital admissions (as of January 17, 2024). ■ More than 1.6 lakh primary healthcare facilities upgraded to **Ayushman Arogya Mandir (erstwhile AB-HWCs)** (as of December 13, 2023). ■ More than 17.4 crore patients availed **e-Sanjeevani** OPD services in Ayushman Arogya Mandir (as of November 3, 2023). ■ 10,000 **Janaushadhi Kendras** across the country, selling medicines at 50-90 per cent cheaper rates compared to market rates (as of November 30, 2023) ■ 16 per cent decline in TB incidence between 2015 and 2022, with 18 per cent reduction in mortality. ■ 1 crore beneficiaries of **Janani Suraksha Yojana** in FY22.

Revamped Education	■ **National Education Policy** introduced in 2020 – structural reform in education ■ **National Curriculum Framework for Foundational Stage (NCF FS)** launched on 20th October 2022. Based on this, **Learning Teaching Material (JaduiPitara)** and Textbooks have been launched in 2023. ■ **PARAKH (Performance Assessment, Review, and Analysis of Knowledge for Holistic Development),** launched in 2023 for setting norms and implementing activities related to student assessment. ■ Scheme for 14,500 PM-SHRI Schools to emerge as model schools for NEP. ■ **NIPUN Bharat Mission** for universal acquisition of foundational literacy and numeracy by 2026-27. ■ Expansion of digital learning through **Swayam Prabha and MOOCs** – 200 channels with more than 13,000 contents produced for telecast in 31 languages. Achievements of **Samagra Shiksha** from 2018-19 to 2023-24.
Largescale Skilling	■ 1.4 crore candidates trained under **PM Kaushal Vikas Yojana** since 2015 (as of December 13, 2023). ■ **Skill India Digital platform** launched in September 2023, bringing all skill initiatives together. ■ 26.9 lakh apprentices engaged under the **National Apprenticeship Promotion Scheme** (as of September 30, 2023). ■ **PM Vishwakarma scheme** launched in September 2023 to provide end-to-end support to artisans and craftspeople, including skill upgradation, collateral-free concessional loans of up to ₹3 lakh

Entrepreneu-rship	■ 1,14,902 **DPIIT-recognized start-ups** across 763 districts of the country (as of October 31, 2023). ■ 44.5 crore loans worth ₹26.1 lakh crore were sanctioned under the **MUDRA Yojana**, with 68 per cent of accounts belonging to women entrepreneurs. ■ Under **PMSVANidhi**, 82.3 lakh loans were sanctioned to over 58 lakh street vendors, with a total value exceeding ₹10,922.4 crore (as of January 11, 2024) ■ Under **DAY-NRLM**, 9.5 crore women mobilised into 87.4 lakh Self-Help Groups under DAY-NRLM (as of December 2023). ■ Under **Stand-Up India**, 2.1 lakh loans have been sanctioned, of which 84 per cent have been sanctioned to women entrepreneurs (as of November 24, 2023).
Basic Amenities	■ 11 crore toilets and 2.3 lakh community toilet complexes were constructed under **Swachh Bharat Mission Grameen** (as of January 11, 2024). ■ 10.8 crore households provided tap water connection under **Jal Jeevan Mission** (as of January 11, 2024). ■ Under **PM-AWAS-Urban and PM-AWAS-Gramin,** 79 lakh and 2.5 crore houses were constructed for the poor in the last 9 years (as of January 8, 2024 and January 11, 2024). ■ 10 crore LPG connections provided under **PM Ujjwala Yojana** since 2016 (as of January 8, 2024) ■ 21.4 crore rural households electrified under **Saubhagya** since 2015 (as of March 31, 2019) ■ **Digital India**: 4.5 lakh common service centres set up in rural areas (as of November 30, 2023)

Social Security	■ 51.4 crore accounts opened under **PM Jan Dhan Yojana** (as of January 3, 2024). ■ 18.5 crore and 41.0 crore enrolments under **PM Jeevan Jyoti Yojana** and **PM Suraksha Beema Yojana**, respectively (as of November 15, 2023). ■ **Atal Pension Yojana** (launched in 2015) total subscriber base has risen to 6.1 crore (as of December 31, 2023). ■ Assured pension for 49.7 lakh unorganised workers enrolled under **PM Shram Yogi Maandhan Yojan**a (as of December 31, 2023).

Women-led development: Tapping the Gender Dividend for India@100

- The passage of the **women's reservation Bill (Nari Shakti Vandan Adhiniyam (NSVA))** in September 2023 coincided with the year of India's G20 Presidency, listing **"women-led development" as one of its six priorities.**
- Globally, rising attention towards women's workforce participation and outcomes followed the award of the **Nobel Prize in Economics to Prof. Claudia Goldin** for her work on key drivers of **gender differences in the labour market.**

Women's representation in government

- Women's representation in government is low not just in India, but globally. A quota in government has been approved in **107 nations**, including **Australia, Germany, the United Arab Emirates, the United Kingdom, and Sweden.**
- **Rwanda, Cuba, Mexico, New Zealand, and the UAE** have the greatest female participation rates in their lower houses, with 50 per cent or more. However, women account for less than 33 per cent of the population in 134 of 185 countries. In addition, 91 countries have less than 25 per cent female involvement. India has approximately 15 per cent.

- As of June 2023, **India ranked 148th out of 193 countries** in terms of the per centage of elected women representatives in national legislatures.

Government Initiatives

- **PM Jan Dhan Yojana:** The proportion of women having bank accounts that they themselves use increased from 53 per cent in 2015-16 to 78.6 per cent in 2019-21.
- **Women-led SHGs** have a positive, statistically significant effect on women's economic, social, and political empowerment.
- **Deendayal Antyodaya Yojana-National Rural Livelihood Mission (DAY-NRLM),** is the government's SHG programme covering nearly 9 crore women through 83 lakh SHGs.
- **Lakhpati Didis:** Recently, the government has targeted the creation of 2 crore 'Lakhpati Didis'(women with annual earnings of ₹1 lakh and more) through skilling SHG members with marketable skills such as plumbing, LED bulb making, and operation of drones and repair, etc.
- **Female participation** has been quite encouraging in the wave of human capital formation through Skill India Mission and Start-up and Stand-Up India.
- Under the **PM Kaushal Vikas Yojana**, over 59 lakh women have been certified, which constitutes more than 40 per cent of the total certified as of June 2022.
- Around 70 per cent of the loans have been sanctioned to women entrepreneurs under **PM Mudra Yojana**, and 80 per cent of the beneficiaries under Stand-Up India are women.
- More than 53 per cent of the beneficiaries of the **Prime Minister's Rural Digital Literacy Campaign (PMGDISHA)** are women as of July 2023.
- **Make life easy for women:**
  - Construction of over 11 crore toilets under 'Swachh Bharat Mission'.

- Clean cooking gas connections to nearly 10.1 crore women below the poverty line under 'Ujjwala Yojana'.
- Connecting over 14.1 crore out of 19.3 crore rural households with tap drinking water connections under 'Jal Jeevan Mission'.

Key-Government interventions for digital empowerment of Women

- **Digital Saksharta Abhiyan:** The Digital Saksharta Abhiyan is a government initiative in India that aims to provide digital literacy training to people in rural areas, including women. The program was launched in 2015 by the Ministry of Electronics and Information Technology as part of the Digital India campaign.
- **Mission Digital Shakti:** Started in 2018, it aims to help women across the nation to raise the **awareness level on the digital front.**
- **National Commission for Women (NCW)** has launched it in collaboration with **CyberPeace Foundation and Meta.**
- It is helping **women in reporting & redressal mechanisms**, data privacy and usage of technology for their benefits.
- **Digital Shakti 4.0:** Digital Shakti 4.0 is focused on making **women digitally skilled** and aware to stand up against any illegal/ inappropriate activity online. It aims to ensure safe cyber spaces for women.
- **Pradhan Mantri Gramin Digital Saksharta Abhiyan (PMGDISHA):** Launched under Digital India programme, it aims to bridge the digital divide specially targeting rural population including the marginalised sections of society, women and girls by covering 6 crore rural households.

- Under **PM AWAS Yojana (Gramin),** 26.6 per cent of the 2.4 crore completed houses are solely in the name of women.
- The emphasis on **"Beti Bachao, Beti Padhao"** has sensitised collective consciousness towards saving, educating, and saving for the girl child (via Sukanya Samriddhi Yojana, a flagship small deposits scheme for financial planning for the girl child. The scheme has more than 3.1 crore accounts to its credit).

The above mentioned initiatives have already begun paying dividends:

- The GER of girls in the schools at the secondary level has increased from 75.5 per cent in (FY15) to 79.4 per cent in FY22.
- The female labour force participation rate (LFPR) rose to 37 per cent in 2022-23 from 23.3 per cent in 2017-18.
- improvement in the sex ratio at birth from 918 in 2014-15 to 933 in 2022-23.
- reduction in maternal mortality rate from 130/lakh live births in 2014-16 to 97/lakh live births in 2018-20 (Figure 3).

FIGURE 3: Female Labour Force Participation Rate (Rural+Urban), Usual Status, 15 years and above

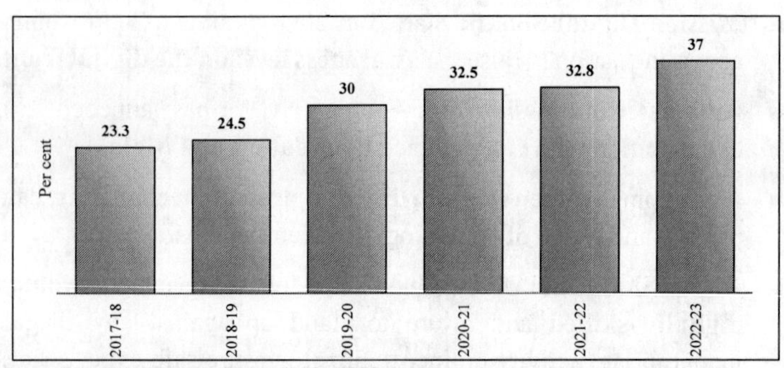

Source: Periodic Labour Force Survey (PLFS), NSSO

Employment situation in the past decade

Over the past decade, India has witnessed a notable transformation in its employment landscape. This evolution results from various factors, including

- economic reforms
- technological advancements
- emphasis on skill development

The slew of structural reforms promoting ease of doing business remains crucial for productive employment generation in the current decade.

- According to the annual **Periodic Labour Force Surveys (PLFS) by the National Statistical Organisation, MoSPI,** the unemployment rate has declined substantially from 6 per cent in 2017-18 (when the first round of the survey was conducted) to 3.2 per cent in 2022-23, a trend observed across male and female workers in rural and urban areas.
- This has been accompanied by a rising **LFPR** from 49.8 per cent in 2017-18 to 57.9 per cent in 2022- 23, driven by a surge in rural female LFPR.
- The labour markets also recovered swiftly from the impact of the pandemic, with the rural areas witnessing a faster-paced resumption.

TABLE 1: Annual Labour Market Indicators
(usual status, age 15 years and above)

		Rural		Urban		Rural + Urban	
		2017-18	2022-23	2017-18	2022-23	2017-18	2022-23
Male	LFPR	76.4	80.2	74.5	74.5	75.8	78.5
	WPR	72.0	78.0	69.3	71.0	71.2	76.0
	UR	5.7	2.7	6.9	4.7	6.1	3.3
Female	LFPR	24.6	41.5	20.4	25.4	23.3	37.0
	WPR	23.7	40.7	18.2	23.5	22.0	35.9
	UR	3.8	1.8	10.8	7.5	5.6	2.9
Person	LFPR	50.7	60.8	47.6	50.4	49.8	57.9
	WPR	48.1	59.4	43.9	47.7	46.8	56.0
	UR	5.3	2.4	7.7	5.4	6.0	3.2

Source: Annual Periodic Labour Force Survey (PLFS)

- **Creation of regular jobs**: The organised sector job market conditions measured by payroll data for **Employees' Provident Fund Organisation (EPFO)** indicate a consistent YoY increase in payroll addition since 2018-19. The EPFO membership numbers (for which older data is available) grew by an impressive 11.3 per cent CAGR between FY14 and FY22. These confirm the creation of regular jobs in India.
- **Gig economy:** With affordable access to the internet and smartphones, the rise of the gig economy has emerged as a noteworthy job generator, employing 77 lakh workers in FY21, as per a NITI Aayog report.

Who is a 'gig worker'?

- Gig workers refer to workers **outside of the traditional employer-employee relationship**.
- There are two groups of gig workers—
  - **Platform workers:** When gig workers use online algorithmic matching platforms or apps to connect with customers, they are called platform workers.
  - **Non-platform workers**: Those who work outside of these platforms are non-platform workers, including construction workers and non-technology-based temporary workers.

A **2022 report by NITI Aayog** estimates that nearly 23.5 million workers will be engaged in the gig economy by 2029.

- **Challenges:** There remain long-existing challenges of formalising a burgeoning workforce, facilitating job creation in sectors that can absorb workers shifting from agriculture, and ensuring social security benefits for those in regular wage/salaried employment.

Rising Youth Employment

- According to the PLFS, youth (age 15-29 years) unemployment rate has declined from 17.8 per cent in 2017-18 to 10 per cent in 2022-23, while youth LFPR has expanded from 38.2 per cent to 44.5 per cent over the same period.
- At the state level, the decline in the youth unemployment rate has been led by the states with a larger share of the young population, such as **Uttar Pradesh** (with 6.9 crore youth as per MoHFW's population estimates for 2021), **Bihar (with 3.5 crore youth), and Madhya Pradesh (with 2.3 crore youth).**
  - For instance, UP's youth unemployment rate has declined from 16.7 per cent in 2017-18 to 7 per cent in 2022-23, accompanied by a rise in youth LFPR from 33.7 per cent to 41.4 per cent in the corresponding period.

- Thus, the states driving the youth bulge are also leading the rise in youth employment.

Rising Female Labour Force Participation Rate

Understanding Women's Role in Economy in India:

- The present contribution of women to the National **GDP** is around **18%.**
- **Sector-wise contribution:**
  - In India, women comprise **48% of the agricultural workforce** and own **only 13% of the land**.
  - Women in India constitute around 20% of the manufacturing workforce and around 30% of the total workforce in the services sector.
  - At present, there are 432 million women of working age in India, out of which 343 million are employed in the **unorganized sector.**
- India has the **3rd largest ecosystem** in terms of Start-ups in the world, and 10% of them have been led by women founders.
  - Also, research shows that ventures started by women are more sustainable in nature.

CHALLENGES FACED BY WORKING WOMEN	IMPACTS
■ **Pay Disparity:** The World Inequality Report of 2022 noted that men earn 82% of the labour income while women earn 18% of it. ■ **Sexual Harassment:** Despite the 2013 Sexual Harassment of Women at Workplace (Prevention, Prohibition and Redressal) Act in place, a data analysis compiled by Complykaro.com, an anti-sexual harassment advisory witnessed a rise in workplace sexual harassment complaints by 27% in March 2022.	■ Lack of women participation makes the skill-set limited. ■ Lesser growth or stagnant growth

- **Pregnancy discrimination**: The **Maternity Benefit Act, Sec. 5(3),** states that a minimum of 14 weeks of paid leaves be provided to a new mother.
  - Yet women face unfair treatment at work like stereotyping, intrusive comments, and even a lack of relevant projects being handed to them.
- **Imposter syndrome**
- **Ignorance and lack of sensitivity**
- Required measures:
  - Improving access to education
  - Providing support services Encouraging women's participation in leadership roles
  - Addressing discrimination and bias
  - Encouraging community participation

- In the new millennium, **India's Female LFPR (FLFPR)** declined measurably, accompanied by a steep rise in the enrollment of females in education.
  - For example, the female GER in senior secondary education more than doubled from 24.5 per cent in 2004-05 to 58.2 per cent in 2021-22, and the female GER in higher education quadrupled from 6.7 per cent in FY2001 to 27.9 per cent in FY21.
- The young cohorts of females are increasingly taking to higher studies, which enables more rewarding workforce participation in the decades to come, thereby actualising **Goldin's U-curve** between FLFPR and education in the Indian context.

Claudia Goldin gave the 'U' shaped **female labour force function curve** and she related it to the level of education and the emergence of the white collar sector jobs. The downward trend in the 'U' was due to rise in incomes because of expansion of markets and shift from farm activities.

- This naturally limits the FLFPR for a country one-fourth of whose population is below 15 years old and more than half of the population is below 30 years old while refining the quality of the future workforce.
- The rise in rural female LFPR has been accompanied by
  - **Contribution to rural production**: Firstly, the rise in rural female employment has been contributed by both own account worker/

employer category (share rising from 19 per cent in 2017-18 to 27.9 per cent in 2022- 23) and the unpaid helper category (share rising from 38.7 per cent to 43.1 per cent, which is a relatively smaller rise), indicating a rising contribution of females to rural production.

- **Structural shift:** Secondly, the rise in the share of agriculture in the rural female workforce from 73.2 per cent in 2017-18 to 76.2 per cent in 2022-23 coincides with a more significant decline in the share of agriculture in the rural male workforce from 55 per cent in 2017-18 to 49.1 per cent in 2022-23. This is plausibly due to men taking up rising opportunities in non-agriculture and women at home filling in for the men on the farm.
- **Skilled agriculture labour**: Thirdly, within the rural female workforce, there has been a structural shift marked by a rising proportion of skilled agriculture labour (up from 48 per cent in 2018-19 to 59.4 per cent in 2022-23) and a decline in the share of elementary agriculture labourers using considerable physical effort, from 23.4 per cent to 16.6 per cent over the same period.

Summing up, youth and female employment have risen steadily in the last six years and are the keystones to utilising India's demographic advantage.

Skill Development and Entrepreneurship

- Recognising the importance of a skilled workforce in a rapidly changing global economy, the government has taken proactive measures to enhance the employability of its citizens.
- **Establishment of a Central Ministry** in 2014
- **National Skill Development Mission and National Policy on Skill Development** and **Entrepreneurship** to improve and streamline the skilling ecosystem
- Under the **National Education Policy 2020,** there is also a special focus on vocational education and skill development.

- **Skill India Mission**, launched in 2015, is central to the skill development landscape in India.
- The growth in youth employment has been coupled with the progress in skill development, with nearly 1.4 crore candidates trained under **PM Kaushal Vikas Yojana** since 2015.
- The recent launch of the **Skill India Digital platform** as the **Digital Public Infrastructure** for the skilling, education, employment, and entrepreneurship ecosystem marks another step towards the "ease of acquiring skill" in India.
- The across-the-board progress in skilling has manifested in India's rising position in **World Skills Competitions,** from 39 in 2011 to 11 in 2022.
- Further, according to **India Skills Report 2023**, the employable per centage of final-year and pre-final-year students has increased from 33.9 per cent in 2014 to 51.3 per cent in 2024.

As the nation continues to invest in its human capital, the positive impact of these skill development initiatives is likely to be felt across sectors, driving economic prosperity and social development.

INDIA'S EXTERNAL SECTOR: SAFELY NAVIGATING THROUGH UNCERTAINTIES

Challenges: sticky inflation, sluggish growth, and mounting fiscal pressures, ongoing geopolitical tensions and the recent surge in shipping costs due to rerouting to avoid security risks in international waters.

Merchandise trade depicted resilience

- **India's exports:** India's exports have been showing remarkable performance, logging record-high levels since FY22, with
  - merchandise exports rising by **more than 50 per cent**

  - services exports by 120 per cent over the past decade (FY13 to FY23)

- The highest-ever merchandise export of USD 451.1 billion was achieved in FY23.

- Though the export mix, in terms of the principal commodity classification of the DGCI&S, has not changed much over the years, there has been progressive diversification in India's export basket, and there is scope for adding more quality and complexity to exports, given the existing capabilities.

- **Export of Services:** In the export of services, India has carved a niche for itself as a knowledge-based economy, as is evident from the fact that software services exports comprise almost half of the service exports consistently.

- An increased presence of **Global Capability Centres** in India during and following the pandemic years is a manifestation of this change.

- The **Department of Telecommunications** issued guidelines for Other Service Providers (OSPs), which promoted the **Work-From-Home culture** in India and extended it to allow **Work-From-Anywhere** in India.

  - The guidelines included provision for the sharing of infrastructure, use of the distributed architecture of **Electronic Private Automatic Branch Exchange (EPABX)** and interconnection.

Comfortable balance on current account

- **Service exports**, with a CAGR of 7.1 per cent during FY12 to FY23, combined with the **CAGR of remittances of 4.5 per cent** during the same period, enabled **India's current account balance** to remain within a **comfortable range**, especially after FY14. The current account deficit (CAD) dropped significantly.

- **Broad-based improvements in both merchandise trade and invisibles** led to this improvement.

- **Remittances**: India is the largest recipient of worker remittances in the world, receiving USD 125 billion in the year 2023.

- These remittances have benefitted from a gradual structural shift in Indian migrants' key destinations from largely low-skilled, informal employment towards high skilled jobs in high-income countries such as the United States, the United Kingdom, and East Asia, aided by a structural shift in qualifications.

> As per the **World Migration Report 2022**, almost 36 per cent of India's remittances are attributable to the high-skilled and largely hightech Indian migrants in the top high-income destinations.

Capital account

- The negative balance on the **current account** is compensated by the positive balance on the capital account, resulting in the accretion of foreign exchange reserves of USD 27 billion since the end of FY23.
- **Stability in the rupee** vis-à-vis **other currencies** during FY24, easing inflationary pressures across the globe and triggering expectations of rate cuts in future, led the **foreign portfolio investors (FPIs)** to increase their exposure to Indian markets.
- A host of measures have been undertaken in recent years.
  - simplification and rationalisation of the FPI regulatory regime
  - permitting FPIs to participate in the currency derivatives segment of a recognised stock exchange
  - invest in units of the REITs, InvITs and Category III Alternative Investment Funds (AIFs)
  - easing exit process for these investors
  - making amendments in the FPI regulations to streamline the onboarding process of the FPIs
  - operationalisation of the online Common Application Form (CAF) for registration with SEBI, allotment of PAN and opening of bank and Demat accounts
- **The Rupee-dollar exchange rate** during the last decade (FY14 to FY23) fluctuated on an average basis in the range of ₹60/USD to ₹80/USD.

- The macroeconomic stability and improvements in India's external position, particularly significant moderation in the CAD and revival of capital flows on the back of a comfortable foreign exchange reserves buffer resulted in stability in the Indian rupee.

- **The foreign exchange reserves** stood at USD 623.2 billion as in December 2023, covering imports of more than ten months.
- **The net IIP (NIIP)** (net claims of non-residents in India) to GDP ratio, which indicates the creditworthiness of a country witnessed a consistent decline over the past decade, i.e., from (-) 18.2 per cent of GDP at end-March 2014 to (-) 11.3 per cent at end-September 2023.
  - A decline in this ratio signals constructive utilisation of financial liabilities in the GDP creation.

> **The international investment position (IIP)** is the **balance sheet of a country's external financial assets and liabilities**. It is an indicator of the degree of financial openness of a country.

Way Forward for the External Sector

On the investment front, with continuous reforms in the FDI policy along with a thrust on improving infrastructure and logistics and facilitating investments through schemes like production-linked incentives, it is expected that the momentum of inflows will be sustained.

CLIMATE ACTION

What is required?

- Achieving high resilient growth while ensuring sustainable and inclusive livelihood options for all remains a priority for the country.
- Access to energy, which powers industry and enables access to education, health and overall social and economic well-being, is vital in achieving our development goals that provide maximum social and economic returns.

What is India's approach?

Recognising the clear priority to development but also accepting the need for contributing to the collective action to address climate change in the context of the **United Nations Framework Convention for Climate Change (UNFCCC)** and the **Paris Agreement**, India has adopted a **comprehensive approach** that addresses adaptation, resilience building and mitigation action as part of its contribution to the global response to climate change despite its low historical contribution to global carbon stock.

- It is worth noting that, per capita, **India will remain a low emitter for quite some time to come.**
- **Nationally Determined Contributions:** India announced its first **NDCs** at the UNFCCC in 2015. These NDCs included
  - an ambition to **reduce the emission intensity** of India's GDP by 33 to 35 per cent by 2030 from the 2005 level
  - achieve about 40 per cent cumulative electric power installed capacity from non-fossil fuel-based energy resources by 2030
  - create an additional carbon sink of 2.5 to 3 billion tonnes of CO_2 equivalent by 2030 through the creation of additional forest and tree cover.
- Against these goals, India has already **met the targets of building non-fossil fuel-installed electricity capacity, reaching 43.9 per cent in November 2023** (up from 32.3 per cent in 2014 and 30.4 per cent in 2004).

IMPORTANT SCHEMES

- Development of Solar Parks and Ultra Mega Solar Power Projects
- Rooftop Solar Scheme
- Green Energy Corridor (GEC)
- Production-Linked-Incentive (PLI) scheme for manufacturing 'High-Efficiency Solar PV Modules' and PLI scheme 'National Programme on Advanced Chemistry Cell (ACC) Battery Storage'
- Smart Meter National Program
- Integrated Power Development Scheme
- Street Lighting National Programme (SNLP)
- Pradhan Mantri Kisan Urja Suraksha Evam Utthan Mahabhiyan (PM-KUSUM)
- Unnat Jyoti by Affordable LEDs for All (UJALA)
- Pradhan Mantri Ujjwala Yojana (PMUY)
- Faster Adoption and Manufacturing of Electric Vehicles (FAME) scheme

- **Carbon sink:** Further, an additional carbon sink of 1.97 billion tonnes of CO_2 equivalent has been created by 2019, which is higher than the 2005 level.
- **LiFE:** India focused on promoting a healthy and sustainable way of living through a mass movement for LiFE – Lifestyle for Environment.
- **National Action Plan on Climate Change (NAPCC):** The strengthened NAPCC has been a prominent intervention for the implementation of India's climate action and comprises nine missions in specific areas of solar energy, energy efficiency, water, sustainable agriculture, Himalayan ecosystem, sustainable habitat, green India, strategic knowledge for climate change, and including the recent Health Mission.
- **National Adaptation Fund for Climate Change**: NAFCC was introduced in 2015-16 to support adaptation action in, among other things, agriculture, water, forestry, livestock, and restoring ecosystems and has been implemented in project mode with 30 projects sanctioned in 27 States and UTs.
- **The Perform Achieve and Trade (PAT) scheme** - an energy savings-based market mechanism - has resulted in savings of about 24.3 million tonnes of Oil Equivalent, translating into avoiding about 105.02 million tonnes of CO_2 emissions by 2022.
- **The Energy Conservation Act was amended in 2022** to pave the way for establishing a domestic carbon market - the **Carbon Credit Trading Scheme (CCTS),** which will further deepen the efforts to incentivise energy saving, reduction and abatement of emissions.
- **National Green Hydrogen Mission**: The Mission was launched in 2023 with a dual objective to boost hydrogen production using renewable energy sources and reduce emissions. The mission is expected to lead to the development of 5 million metric tonnes (MMT) of green hydrogen production capacity per annum by 2030.

> Hydrogen is a promising fuel that can be used for long-duration storage of renewable energy, replacement of fossil fuels in industry, and clean transportation.

How government dealt with climate consciousness while focusing on the development objective?

- Building resilience and adaptive capacity to climate change impacts require actions on multiple fronts.
- The government of India's policies and initiatives to achieve high economic growth, substantially improve the standard of living, ensure food and water security, manage disaster risks and create resilient infrastructure, improve health and social infrastructure, and take steps to conserve biodiversity and natural resources are some of the measures to enhance resilience.
- These include
  - National Clean Air Programme (NCAP)
  - Namami Gange Programme, Atal Bhujal Yojana (ATAL JAL)
  - Compensatory Afforestation Fund Act 2016
  - Pradhan Mantri Krishi Sinchayee Yojana (PMKSY)
  - National Bamboo Mission (NBM)
  - National Coastal Mission
  - National Health Mission
  - National Cyclone Risk Mitigation Project
  - National Disaster Management Plan 2019
  - Mangrove Initiative for Shoreline Habitats and Tangible Income (MISHTI)

International Initiatives for climate change

In addition to ambitious domestic actions, several international initiatives since 2014, such as

- International Solar Alliance (ISA)
- Coalition for Disaster Resilient Infrastructure (CDRI)
- Infrastructure for Resilient Island States (IRIS)
- Green Grids Initiative-One Sun One World One Grid (GGIOSOWOG)

- India also co-leads the **Leadership Group for Industry Transition (LeadIT)** with Sweden.

LeadIT 2.0:

- In COP28, the second phase, LeadIT 2.0, was launched, marking a joint commitment by member countries and companies to shape policy frameworks and international cooperation for an inclusive industry transition.
  - The group will focus on global dialogue, technology collaboration, and fostering industry transition partnerships in this phase.

Way forward (the right climatic strategy)

Development is key in building resilience and enabling effective mitigation action as, in the medium to long run, development would generate resources and capacity for effective climate action. However, the current global approach to climate change is set on a course that runs the risk of making the low-income status of several nations permanent. Globally, there is a need to "strike the right balance between development and emissions mitigation", and that begins with the realisation that wishing away the trade-off is the wrong place to start.

India, at the 26th session of the **United Nations Framework Convention on Climate Change (COP26)** in November, 2021, announced its target to achieve **net zero by 2070.**

On its part, the government of India holds the achievement of the developmental priorities as central to this effort. The goal of reaching **net zero by 2070** and enhanced NDC for 2030 is being pursued with a wide array of policy and regulatory measures, as well as incentives to weave production and consumption patterns in the country with mindful and deliberate utilisation instead of mindless and destructive consumption - under **Mission LiFE.**

Outlook

Ten years ago, **India was the 10th largest economy in the world**, with a GDP of USD 1.9 trillion at current market prices. Today, it is the **5th largest with a GDP of USD 3.7 trillion (est. FY24),** despite the pandemic and despite inheriting an economy with macro imbalances and a broken financial sector. This ten-year journey is marked by several reforms, both substantive and incremental, which have significantly contributed to the country's economic progress.

In the next three years, **India is expected to become the third-largest economy in the world**, with a GDP of USD 5 trillion. The government has, however, set a higher goal of becoming a **'developed country' by 2047.**

PRELIMS MCQs

Q1: Consider the following statement with reference to twin balance sheet problem:

Statement I

- The problem of overleveraged companies and bad-loan-encumbered banks in the corporate and banking sectors' balance sheets is known as twin balance sheet problem.

Statement II

- The recapitalization and merger of Public Sector Banks (PSB) and Amendment of the SARFAESI Act 2002 to enacting the Insolvency and Bankruptcy Code 2016 (IBC) have helped clean up the balance sheets of banks and corporates.

Which of the following is correct in respect of the above statements?

(a) Both Statement-I and Statement-II are correct and Statement-II is the correct explanation for Statement-I

(b) Both Statement-I and Statement-II are correct and Statement-II is not the correct explanation for Statement-I

(c) Statement-I is incorrect but Statement-II is correct

(d) Statement-I is correct but Statement-II is incorrect

Q2: Consider the following statements

1. Nominal GDP is the value of GDP at current prices, while real GDP is the value of GDP at constant prices.
2. Gross Value Added (GVA) is the value of output minus the value of intermediate consumption, while No Value Added (NVA) is the value of output minus the value of intermediate consumption and depreciation.
3. GDP at market prices is the sum of gross value added by all producers plus taxes on products minus subsidies on

products, while GDP at factor cost is the sum of gross value added by all producers plus taxes on production minus subsidies on production.

How many of the given statements are correct?

(a) Only 1 (b) Only 2

(c) All 3 (d) None

Q3: Consider the following statements with respect to global capability centers (GCC):

1. The availability of a highly-skilled workforce capable of research and innovation, using high-end technology, and possessing managerial skills has led to the setting up of GCC in India

2. GCCs account for more than 1 per cent of India's GDP

3. Bangalore is the top destination of GCC

How many of the given statements are correct?

(a) Only 1 (b) Only 2

(c) All 3 (d) None

Q4: Consider the following statements with reference to currency devaluation:

1. Currency devaluation makes exports cheaper for foreign buyers, increasing their demand and quantity.

2. Currency devaluation makes exports cheaper for domestic sellers, increasing their supply and quantity.

3. Currency devaluation does not affect the income elasticity of exports, as it only depends on the nature and quality of the goods

4. Currency devaluation improves the balance of trade, as it increases the value of exports and decreases the value of imports.

How many of the given statements are correct?

(a) Only 1 (b) Only 2

(c) Only 3 (d) None

Q5: Consider the following statements with respect to monetary policy:

1. The principal tool of monetary policy employed by RBI is Bank rate.
2. The main objective of monetary policy is price stability
3. Consumer price Index is the main indicator targeted by RBI

How many of the given statements are correct?

(a) Only 1 (b) Only 2

(c) All 3 (d) None

Q6: Consider the following statements:

Statement I

- The macro vulnerability index is released by the International Monetary Fund (IMF) yearly.

Statement II

- This Index adds together the rate of inflation, current account deficit, and fiscal deficit of a country.

Which one of the following is correct in respect of the above statements?

(a) Both Statement-I and Statement-II are correct, and Statement-II is the correct explanation for Statement-I.

(b) Both Statement-I and Statement-II are correct, and Statement-II is not the correct explanation for Statement-I.

(c) Statement I is correct, but Statement II is incorrect.

(d) Statement I is incorrect, but Statement II is correct.

Q7: Consider the following statements:

Statement I: The RBI increased the policy repo rate under the liquidity adjustment facility progressively from 4 per cent in April 2022 to 6.5 per cent till February 2023.

Statement II: This was the act under RBI's supportive monetary policy to ensure that inflation aligns with the target while supporting growth.

Which one of the following is correct in respect of the given statements?

(a) Both Statement-I and Statement-II are correct, and Statement-II is the correct explanation for Statement-I.

(b) Both Statement-I and Statement-II are correct, and Statement-II is not the correct explanation for Statement-I.

(c) Statement I is correct, but Statement II is incorrect.

(d) Statement I is incorrect, but Statement II is correct.

Q8: Consider the following statements:

1. The Union government expenditure on social services has increased from FY12 to FY23.
2. The sole aim of the government to increase social expenditure is to elevate the standard of Living.
3. The Output-Outcome Monitoring Framework for major central sector and centrally sponsored schemes were adopted to shift towards universalization of basic amenities.

How many of the statements given above is/are correct?

(a) Only 1 (b) Only 2

(c) All 3 (d) None

Q9: With respect to the Swavalamban Scheme, launched in 2010-11, consider the following statements:

1. It was launched as a co-contributory scheme for old age pension for unorganised workers.
2. The existing Swavalamban beneficiaries were automatically migrated to Atal Pension Yojana (APY) in 2015-16.

Which of the above statements is/are *incorrect*?

(a) Only 1

(b) Only 2

(c) Both 1 and 2

(d) Neither 1 nor 2

Q10: Consider the following statements regarding the Multi-dimensional Poverty in India:

Statement I

- According to a NITI Aayog report, 13.5 crore Indians escaped multidimensional poverty between 2015-16 and 2019-21.

Statement II

- The reason for poverty reduction was a consistent decline in out-of-pocket health expenditure.

Which one of the following is correct in respect of the above statements?

(a) Both Statement-I and Statement-II are correct, and Statement-II is the correct explanation for Statement-I.

(b) Both Statement-I and Statement-II are correct, and Statement-II is not the correct explanation for Statement-I.

(c) Statement I is correct, but Statement II is incorrect.

(d) Statement I is incorrect, but Statement II is correct.

Q11: Consider the following:

1. Affordable Healthcare
2. Revamped Education
3. Skilling
4. Entrepreneurship
5. Social Security
6. Housing for all

How many among the above are broad aims under the New Welfare Approach by the government?

(a) Only 3 (b) Only 4

(c) Only 5 (d) All 6

Q12: With reference to 'Lakhpati Didis', which among the following is correct?

(a) The women with annual earnings of ₹1 lakh and more through skilling SHG members with marketable skills.

(b) They are equipped for handling stock markets and exploring banking policies.

(c) They are part of the PM Kaushal Vikas Yojana.

(d) Both (a) and (c) are true.

Q13: Consider the following:

1. Promoting ease of doing business
2. Technological advancement
3. Skilling
4. Piped drinking water
5. Clean cooking fuel

How many of the above factors pushed the growth of Female labour force participation as per the current employment data?

(a) Only 2 (b) Only 3

(c) Only 4 (d) All 5

Q14: Consider the following statements:

1. Worker remittances are part of India's capital account.
2. Despite global shocks, India's merchandise trade balance improved in the year 2023.
3. India's software services exports comprise almost half of its service exports.
4. Merchandise exports and imports include only tangible goods and exclude services.

How many of the above statements is/are correct?

(a) Only 1 (b) Only 2

(c) Only 3 (d) All 4

Q15: Consider the following statements:

1. India's DPI, also referred to as India Stack, has enabled online, paperless, and cashless digital access to various public and private services.
2. The India Stack consists of three interconnected layers -The Identity Layer (Aadhaar), the Payments Layer (Unified

Payments Interface, Aadhaar Payments Bridge, Aadhaar Enabled Payment Service) and the Data Layer (Account Aggregator).

Which of the following is correct in respect of the above statements?

(a) Only 1 (b) Only 2

(c) Both 1 and 2 (d) Neither 1 nor 2

ANSWERS									
1. (b)	**2. (c)**	**3. (c)**	**4. (b)**	**5. (b)**	**6. (b)**	**7. (a)**	**8. (b)**	**9. (d)**	**10. (c)**
11. (c)	**12. (a)**	**13. (d)**	**14. (c)**	**15. (c)**					

*****

MAINS PRACTICE QUESTIONS

Q1: Explain the significance of capital expenditure (CapEx) in government spending and its impact on the long-term development and productivity of an economy.

Q2: Examine the importance of primary agricultural credit co-operatives and analyse the extent to which budgetary provisions to them would boost the agricultural sector.

Q3: Explain how start-up ecosystem in India will be boosted through the provisions of Union Budget converging priority sectors for inclusive and equitable economic growth?

Q4: Explore the long-term implications of the gig economy on Indian Economy. Highlight the potential shifts in workforce dynamics, employment relationships, and the overall labour market landscape.

Q5: Analyze the contribution of the private sector in promoting formal employment.

Q6: Discuss the challenges and opportunities associated with attracting and managing FDI inflows.

Q7: Discuss how food processing contributes to improving nutritional security. Highlight the fortification of processed foods and innovations in creating nutritious and accessible food products.

Q8: Evaluate government initiatives and policies aimed at enhancing the production of top crops.

Q9: Assess the significance of participation in global value chains for a country's economic development.

Q10: Examine how global economic crises, such as the financial crisis of 2008, impact a country's external sector.

Q11: Besides the push to physical infrastructure, emphasis on public digital infrastructure is the key to enhance the economic potential of individuals and businesses. Discuss.

Q12: Identify the growth magnets that will propel India's growth in the ongoing decade and give reasons for their contribution.

Q13: Examine the evolving significance of the Non-Banking Financial Company (NBFC) sector within the Indian financial system.

Q14: Insurance, an integral part of the financial sector, plays a significant role in economic development. Comment

Q15: Analyze the role of central banks in addressing economic challenges, including the rapid rate hikes and their effects on inflation and financial conditions.

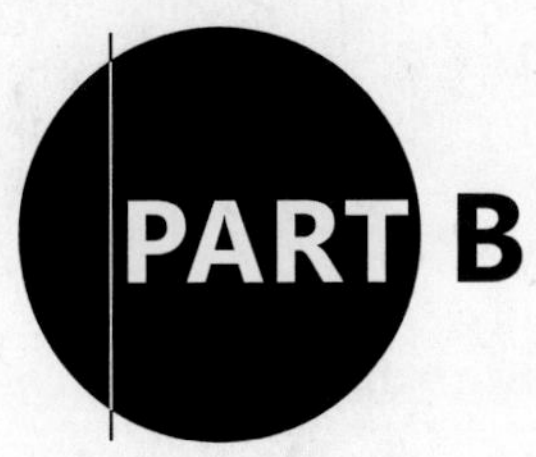

PREVIOUS YEARS' ECONOMIC SURVEY: SUMMARY

KEY-TERMS

- **Economic Slowdown:**

  An economic slowdown occurs when the rate of economic growth slows in an economy. It can be caused by a variety of factors, including declining consumer and business confidence, rising unemployment, and slowing global trade.

- **Invisibles in Economy:**

  The invisible balance or balance of trade on services is that part of the balance of trade that refers to services and other products that do not result in the transfer of physical objects. Examples include consulting services, shipping services, tourism, and patent license revenues.

- **Eight Core Index:**

  The index measures combined and individual performance of production in selected eight core industries viz. Coal, Crude Oil, Natural Gas, Refinery Products, Fertilizers, Steel, Cement and Electricity.

- **Capacity Utilisation:**

  Capacity utilization rate measures the percentage of an organization's potential output that is actually being realized.

- **Emerging Market Economy:**

  An emerging market economy refers to a country that is in the process of developing its economy to become more advanced.

- **Agriculture Infrastructure Fund:**

  Agriculture Infrastructure Fund is a central sector scheme which enables a financing facility of ₹1 lakh crore for funding agriculture infrastructure projects at farm-gate and aggregation points such as farmer producer organizations, primary agricultural cooperatives, startups and entrepreneurs in the agriculture sector.

■ Gross Fixed Capital Formation:

Gross fixed capital formation is a macroeconomic concept used in official national accounts such as the United Nations System of National Accounts, National Income and Product Accounts and the European System of Accounts. Gross Fixed Capital Formation (GFCF) in the Indian economy which has increased from ₹ 32.78 lakh crore (constant 2011-12 prices) in 2014-15 to ₹ 54.35 lakh crore in 2022-23 (provisional estimates).

■ Marginal Costs of Funds-based Lending Rate (MCLR):

Marginal Cost of Fund-based Lending Rate (MCLR) is the minimum lending rate below which a bank is not permitted to lend. MCLR replaced the earlier base rate system to determine the lending rates for commercial banks. RBI implemented MCLR on 1 April 2016 to determine rates of interests for loans.

■ PMI:

The Purchasing Managers' Index (PMI) is an index of the prevailing direction of economic trends in the manufacturing and service sectors. It consists of a diffusion index that summarizes whether market conditions, as viewed by purchasing managers, are expanding, staying the same, or contracting.

■ Account Aggregator Framework:

The Account Aggregator (AA) is an NBFC that collects the financial information of customers and transfers them from one financial institution to another, after the explicit consent of the customers.

■ Free Trade Agreements:

A Free Trade Agreement (FTA) is an agreement between two or more countries where the countries agree on certain obligations that affect trade in goods and services, and protections for investors and intellectual property rights, among other topics.

- **Sovereign External Debt:**

  Sovereign debt is debt issued by a country's government in order to borrow money.

- **Dated Securities:**

  Dated government securities are debt instruments issued by the government that offer investment options with a long-term maturity period.

- **Green Bond:**

  A green bond is a type of fixed-income instrument that is specifically earmarked to raise money for climate and environmental projects.

- **Currency Depreciation:**

  Currency depreciation is when a currency falls in value compared to other currencies.

*****

PREVIOUS YEARS' ECONOMIC SURVEY

1. STATE OF THE ECONOMY 2022-23: COMPLETE RECOVERY

Introduction

The global economic shocks were severe and hit the economy thrice since 2020. It all started with the pandemic-induced contraction of the global output, followed by the Russia-Ukraine conflict leading to a worldwide surge in inflation. To curb the menace of economic slowdown and inflation, the Federal Reserve (Central bank) responded with significant policy measures.

With the increase in tightening policy measures taken by banks across world, the debt of the non-financial sector has risen with **persistent inflation** lowering the global growth as indicated by the World economic outlook report for the year 2022 and 2023. Amid such impacts over the developed and developing economies, India's economy appears to have moved on after its encounter with the pandemic, staging a full recovery in FY22 ahead of many nations and positioning itself to ascend to the pre-pandemic growth path in FY23.

> **Note:** To support economic growth, the expansion of public digital platforms and path-breaking measures such as **PM Gati Shakti, the National Logistics Policy, and the Production-Linked Incentive** schemes will help to boost manufacturing output.

The global economy battles through a unique set of challenges

- **Persistent challenges from previous millennium**: The Present scenario was compared to last century's event when the two world wars took place with the deadly Spanish flu spread with the great depression. The events which are in process to get recovered includes East Asian crisis, global financial crisis, trade tensions between the super-powers. The steps taken were to curb the coming crisis situation.
- **The string of factors contributing to economic slowdown:** As the global economy was recovering from the pandemic-induced output contraction, the Russia-Ukraine conflict, Israel-Hamas Conflict, Red Sea crisis broke out. They all triggered a swing in commodity prices and, thus, accelerating existing inflationary pressures.
- **Counter-effects of monetary tightening to rein in inflation**: As the Central banks took the monetary operations to curb the inflation and effects; it counter attacked the growth regime of developing nations. This leads to rising sovereign bond yields, and depreciation of most currencies against the US dollar.
- **Global stagflation**: Nations felt compelled to protect their respective economic space, slowed cross-border trade, which posed the fourth challenge to growth with China's tighten policy enabled crisis.
- **The loss of education and income-earning opportunities:** The next challenge was a consequence of the several challenges being faced by the nations i.e. unemployment and job losses.
- **Impacts of supply chain disruption:** The conflict caused the prices of critical commodities such as crude oil, natural gas, fertilisers, and wheat to soar. This strengthened the inflationary pressures that the global economic recovery had triggered, backed by massive fiscal stimuli and ultra-accommodative monetary policies undertaken to limit the output contraction in 2020.
- **Inflation in advanced economies:** The advanced economies accounted for most of the global fiscal expansion and monetary easing, breached historical highs, with rising commodity prices in the Emerging Market Economies (EMEs) led to higher inflation rates.

The challenges mentioned earlier in the same text leads to impacts such as:

- Rising inflation and monetary tightening led to a slowdown in global output beginning in the second half of 2022.
- The **global PMI composite index** has been in the contractionary zone since August 2022, while the yearly growth rates of global trade, retail sales, and industrial production have significantly declined in the second half of 2022.

India's Economic Resilience and Growth Drivers

- **India's growth projections:** Despite strong global headwinds and tighter domestic monetary policy, if India is still expected to grow between 6.5 and 7.0 per cent, and that too without the advantage of **a base effect**. It is estimated to be a reflection of India's underlying economic resilience; of its ability to recoup, renew and re-energise the growth drivers of the economy.
- **Real growth drivers:** India's resilience can be boosted by its domestic stimulus and manufacturing and investment activities consequently gained traction. Private consumption can be one among the factors contributing to the growth.
- **Boost in demand and consumption patterns:** RBI's most recent survey of consumer confidence released in December 2022 pointed to improving sentiment with respect to current and prospective employment and income conditions.
- **Investment in Construction sector:** Apart from housing, construction activity, in general, has significantly risen in FY23 as the much-enlarged capital budget (Capex) of the central government and its public sector enterprises is rapidly being deployed.
- **Investment in manufacturing**: While an increase in **export demand, rebound in consumption, and public capex** have contributed to a recovery in the investment/manufacturing activities of the corporates, their stronger balance sheets have also played a big part equal measure to realising their spending plans.
- **Equivalent banking activities**: The year-on-year growth of credits triggered by their improved financial health will implement the better economic stance in the coming times. At the end of March 2018, gross non-performing loans of banks had touched 11.6 per cent. But,

by September 2023, bad loans had fallen to 3.2 per cent as per the RBI's report on trends and Progress of Banking in India.

FIGURE 1: Declining Gross Non-Performing Assets of SCBs
(as % of Gross Advances)

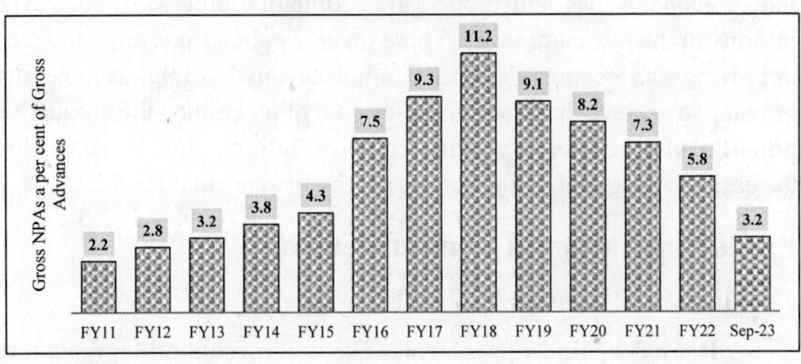

Source: RBI

- **Maintaining growth indicators for banking sector:** The Non-Performing Assets (NPAs) must be recovered with stringent rules against defaulters by Insolvency and Bankruptcy Board of India (IBBI).
- **Adequate budgetary support**: At the same time, the government has been providing adequate budgetary support for keeping the PSBs well-capitalized, ensuring that their Capital Risk-Weighted Adjusted Ratio (CRAR) remains comfortably above the threshold levels of adequacy.

FIGURE 2: Per Capita Real Gross National Income

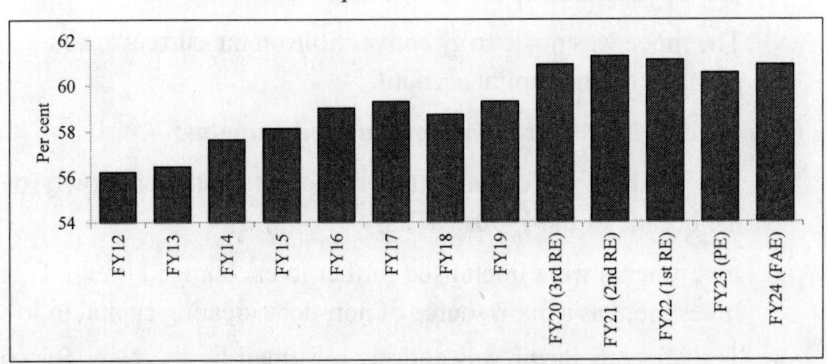

Source: NSO, MoSPI

Note: RE stands for Revised Estimates, PE for Provisional Estimates and FAE for First Advance Estimates

2. INDIA'S MEDIUM-TERM GROWTH OUTLOOK: WITH OPTIMISM AND HOPE

Introduction

Indian economy has undergone a transformative process of New Age reforms in the last eight years. These diverse policies converge towards improving the economy's overall efficiency and lifting its potential growth. To achieve the **broader policy goal** of unleashing the productive **potential of the economy and its people**, the reforms aimed at enhancing the ease of living and doing business at the fundamental level.

Product and Capital Market Reforms

- **Initiation of the reforms - 1991:**
  - **Reason behind the reforms**: The **macroeconomic imbalances** of the late 1980s and early 1990s with high **combined deficit** of the central and state governments, elevated **inflationary pressures,** and large and unsustainable **current account deficit (CAD)** led to a balance of payments crisis in the Indian economy.
  - **Measures taken to liberalise:** Import licensing on almost all intermediate inputs and capital goods were removed, and the entry restrictions for firms were simplified. **Monopoly of public sector** over the many sectors was done away with and the reforms initiated the automatic approval policy for **FDI up to 51 per cent.**
  - The **exchange rate** was made flexible and the currency was **allowed to depreciate** to the level necessary to maintain competitiveness.
  - The rupee was made **fully convertible** on the current account and partially on the capital account.
- **Continuity in Reforms with a Renewed Impetus:**
  - The product and capital market reforms continued slowly over the decade of the 1990s.
  - Investments were liberalised further to encourage Foreign Direct Investment as a main source of non-debt-creating capital inflows.
  - The telecom sector was entirely reformed by the New Telecom Policy 1999.

- Government initiatives brought boost to the IT sector.
- The government set up a dedicated Ministry to take this agenda forward.
- It sold equity stakes in some CPSEs and privatised companies such as **Maruti Udyog, Hindustan Zinc, Bharat Aluminium Company, and Videsh Sanchar Nigam Limited.**
- Focused on economic connectivity was made **via 'Golden Quadrilateral'.**
- Fiscal Responsibility and Budget Management (FRBM) Act was passed to address the historic highs of the combined deficits of the Government.
- The SARFAESI Act allowed banks and financial institutions to recover their dues by proceeding against the secured assets of the borrower/guarantor without the intervention of the court/ tribunals.

■ **One-Off Shocks Overshadowed The Reforms of 1998-2002:**

- The period of these reforms also witnessed a series of domestic and global shocks, which subdued investor confidence.
- After India's nuclear test led to a sharp decline in capital flows to India during the months following the nuclear tests.
- The period between 2000 and 2002 also witnessed **two successive droughts.**

TABLE 1: Occurrence, Number of People Affected and Damages of Droughts in India Between 2000 and 2002

Date	**Location**	Numbers
Apr. 2000	Gujarat, Rajasthan, Madhya Pradesh, Andhra Pradesh, Orissa, Maharashtra	Affected- 9 crore; Damage- US$588,000,000
Nov. 2000	Mahasamund, Raipur, Kawardha, Rajnandgaon, Durg districts (Chhattisgarh region)	
May. 2001	New Delhi, Rajasthan, Gujarat, Orissa	20 deaths
Jul. 2002	Uttar Pradesh, Madhya Pradesh, Rajasthan, Punjab, Haryana, Delhi, Karnataka, Kerala, Nagaland, Orissa, Chhattisgarh, Himachal Pradesh, Gujarat, Maharashtra, Andhra Pradesh, Tamil Nadu	Affected-30 crore; Damage- US$910,721,000
Source: Samra, J. S., 2004. "Review and analysis of drought monitoring, declaration and management in India,"IWMI Working PapersH035617, International Water Management Institute. (https://www.preventionweb. net/files/1868_VL102135.pdf)		

- Though all these factors overshadowed the immediate impact of reforms undertaken by the government then, they laid the groundwork and prepared the Indian economy structurally to participate in the Global Boom which followed soon after.

- **India's Participation in The Global Boom of 2003-08:**
  - The economic growth during the period was supported by **strong capital inflows,** which indicated favourable domestic and external factors.
  - Some of these included sustained momentum in **domestic economic activity, better corporate performance, a conducive investment climate, positive sentiments for India as a preferred investment destination, and encouraging global liquidity conditions/interest rates.**

Reforms for New India – Sabka Saath Sabka Vikaas

- The reforms undertaken before 2014 primarily catered to **product and capital market** space.

FIGURE 3: Underlying Framework for Reforms for a New India

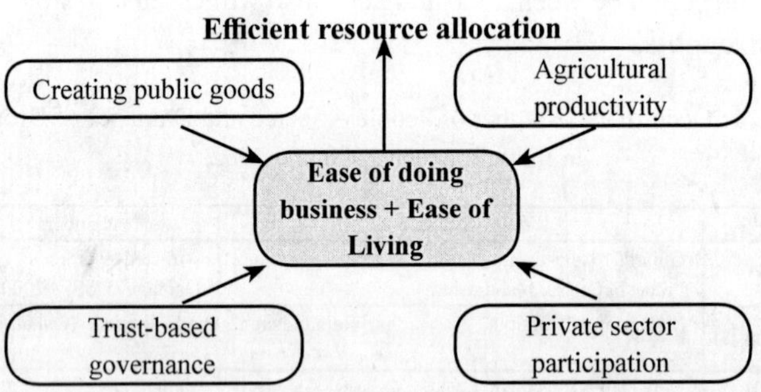

- With an underlying emphasis on enhancing the **ease of living and doing business** and improving economic efficiency the government came up with broad principles on reforms and they were creating public goods, adopting trust-based governance, co-partnering with the private sector for development, and improving agricultural productivity.

- This approach reflects a **paradigm shift in the growth and development** strategy of the government, with the emphasis shifting towards **building partnerships amongst various stakeholders** in the development process, where each contributes to and reaps the development benefits **(Sabka Saath, Sabka Vikaas).**

Phases of Reforms

- **Creating public goods to enhance opportunities, efficiencies and ease of living:** Introducing infrastructure-intensive policymaking in India has led to cushioning economic growth when the non-financial corporate sector was unable to invest due to balance sheet troubles. India built 74 airports in the first 67 years after independence. It doubled that number in the last nine years.
  - The dedicated programs for road connectivity (**Bharatmala), port infrastructure (Sagarmala), electrification, railways upgradation, and operationalizing new airports/air routes (UDAN)** have significantly improved the physical infrastructure in the last few years.

> With the **National Infrastructure Pipeline (NIP)** in 2019 and the **National Monetization Pipeline** in 2021, a strong baseline for infrastructure creation and development has been put in place, providing a multitude of opportunities for foreign investment and engagement.

  - The government is also giving emphasis on developing **digital public infrastructure known as Indiastack** during the last few years which has been the game changer in enhancing the economic potential of **individuals and businesses.**

> **The India Stack consists of three interconnected layers:** The Identity Layer (Aadhaar), the Payments Layer (Unified Payments Interface, Aadhaar Payments Bridge, Aadhaar Enabled Payment Service) and the Data Layer (Account Aggregator). The value of transactions conducted on the UPI platform has increased multifold from ₹0.07 lakh crore in FY17 to ₹143.4 lakh crore in FY24 (April-December 2023

FIGURE 4: Union Government's Capital Expenditure as a per cent of GDP on the Rise

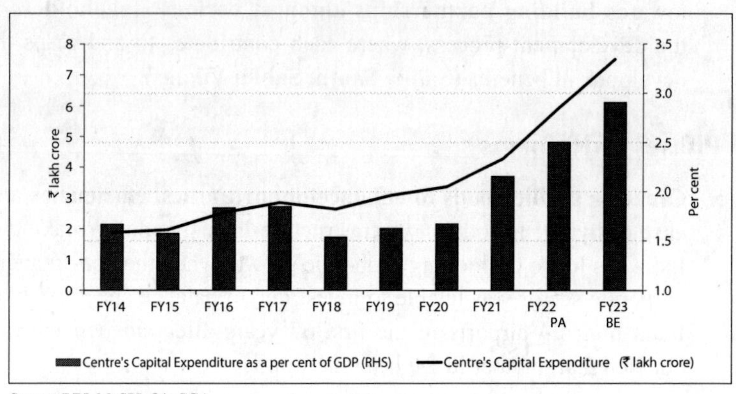

Source: RBI, MoSPI, O/o CGA

Trust-based Governance:

- Building trust between the government and the citizens/businesses unleashes efficiency gains through improved **investor sentiment, better ease of doing business, and more effective governance.**
- Simplification of regulatory frameworks through reforms such as the **Insolvency and Bankruptcy Code (IBC)** and the **Real Estate (Regulation and Development) Act (RERA)** have made doing business in India an investor-friendly.
- To enhance doing business government has decriminalised minor economic offences under the Companies Act of 2013.
- Furthermore, a trust-based approach towards compliance builds entrepreneurs' faith in corporate institutions and motivates them to adopt fairer and more transparent business practices.

Promoting the private sector as a co-partner in the development:

- A fundamental principle behind the government's policy in the post-2014 period has been the engagement with the private sector as a partner in the development process.

- The **privatisation of Air India** was particularly significant for re-igniting the privatisation drive.
- The **New Public Sector Enterprise Policy** for Aatmanirbhar Bharat has thus been introduced to realise higher efficiency gains by minimising the presence of the government in the PSEs to only a few strategic sectors.

Initiatives of government to enhance investment includes:

- **Aatmanirbhar Bharat** and **Make in India Programmes** to enhance India's manufacturing capabilities and exports across the industries.
- Sector-specific **Production Linked Incentives (PLI)** have been introduced in the aftermath of the pandemic to incentivise domestic and foreign investments and to develop global champions in the manufacturing industry.

Enhancing productivity in agriculture:

- Policies such as **Soil Health Cards, the Micro irrigation Fund, and organic and natural farming** have helped the farmers optimise resource use and reduce the cultivation cost.
- The **promotion of Farmer Producer Organisations (FPOs)** and the **National Agriculture Market (e-NAM)** extension Platform have empowered farmers, enhanced their resources, and enabled them to get good returns.

All these measures are directed towards supporting the growth in agricultural productivity and sustaining its contribution to overall economic growth in the medium term.

Growth Magnets in this Decade (2023-2030)

- After a long **period of balance sheet repair** in the financial and corporate sector, the **financial cycle** will improve and move upward as estimated for the coming decade.
- As the **health and economic shocks** of the pandemic and the spike in commodity prices in 2022 wear off, the Indian economy is thus well placed to grow at its potential in the coming decade.

TABLE 2: A Parallel Between the Periods: 1998-2002 and 2014-2022

1998-2002	2014-2022
Shocks to the economy	
■ Nuclear device testing 1998; sanctions followed	■ Period of Banking, Non-Banking and Non-Financial Corporate Sector Balance-sheet stress
■ Banking and Corporate Sector deleveraging and repairing balance-sheets ■ Two successive droughts ■ Technology bust; US recession and 09/11 attack	■ Unprecedented pandemic shock followed by inflation global commodity price shock followed by tightening of financial conditions
Structural reforms in the economy	
■ Interest rate deregulation ■ Privatisation ■ Asset Recovery for banks ■ Infrastructure (Golden quadrilateral) ■ FRBM Act	■ Unique Identity ■ Financial Inclusion ■ GST leading to formalisation ■ Insolvency & Bankruptcy Code ■ Privatisation ■ Tax rates rationalisation and tax administration reforms ■ Decriminalisation of offences ■ Vaccines roll-out ■ Expenditure Management Reforms ■ Aatmanirbhar Bharat ■ Public Digital Infrastructure
Growth returns	
■ One-off shocks delayed the growth returns	■ Balance sheets strengthened in the financial sector; the corporate sector deleveraged by about 30 percentage points (Non-financial private sector debt to GDP ratio)
■ Once shocks faded away, structural reforms paid growth dividends from 2003 onwards	■ Emphasis on macro-economic stability while dealing with global shocks

- The **digitalisation reforms** and the resulting efficiency gains in terms of greater **formalisation, higher financial inclusion, and more economic opportunities**. It will be the second most important driver of India's economic growth in the medium term.
- The **productivity-enhancing reforms** along with the **Government's Skilling initiatives** will also help unleash the benefits of the demographic dividend in the coming years.
- The **evolving geo-political situation** also presents an opportunity for India to benefit from the diversification of **global supply chains**.

UNCTAD, in one of its reports, shows that '**reshoring, diversification, and regionalisation will drive the restructuring of global value chains in the coming years**'.

- It is optimistic that India will achieve an average of **6.5 per cent real GDP growth** in the medium term.

Important Schemes and Initiatives:

- Port infrastructure (Sagarmala)
- UDAN scheme
- National Infrastructure Pipeline (NIP)
- PM-Jan Dhan Yojana
- Open Network for Digital Commerce (ONDC)
- PM SVANidhi Scheme
- PM Gati Shakti

3. FISCAL DEVELOPMENTS: REVENUE RELISH

Introduction

In India, particularly when all economic activities had reached a standstill, fiscal policy was instrumental in providing a safety net to the vulnerable, reviving the economy by boosting demand, and addressing certain domestic supply-side constraints through public investments and sustained structural reforms.

Performance of Union Government Expenditure

- **Pragmatic expenditure policy of re-prioritisation:** During the pandemic of 2021, the total expenditure of the Union Government in FY21 rose to 17.7 per cent of GDP, higher than the previous 5-year average of 12.8 per cent of GDP. In the subsequent year, FY22, the total Union Government expenditure was brought down to 16 per cent of GDP (PA), and a more significant proportion of this accrued to capital expenditure. **The capital expenditure by the Centre has**

steadily increased from a long-term average of 1.7 per cent of GDP (FY09 to FY20) to 2.5 per cent of GDP in FY22 PA. This development has to be seen in the background of Government of India focusing on capital expenditure which would make way for future economic development rather than revenue expenditure and appeasing the people.

- **Capex-led growth to bring back animal spirits and manage debt levels:** The Government of India had budgeted an unprecedented ₹7.5 lakh crore of Capital Expenditure for FY23, of which more than 59.6 per cent has been spent from April to November 2022. During this period, capital expenditure registered a YoY growth of over 60 per cent, much higher than the long-term average growth of 13.5 per cent recorded in the corresponding period from FY16 to FY20. Increase in capital expenditure indicates making ground which can be used for economic gains by animal spirited individuals.
- **Geopolitical developments stretched the Revenue Expenditure requirements:** With the winding up of the pandemic-related support, the revenue expenditure of the Union government was brought down from 15.6 per cent of GDP in the pandemic year FY21 to 13.5 per cent of GDP in FY22 PA. Due to sudden outbreak of geopolitical conflict, the Union Government has sought an additional ₹80,000 crore for the expenditure towards food subsidy and additional allocation under **Pradhan Mantri Garib Kalyan Anna Yojana (PMGKAY)** and ₹1.09 lakh crore for fertiliser subsidy required during the year. As a result, the revenue expenditure from April to November 2022 has grown by over 10 per cent on a YoY basis.
- **Interest payments of receipts** went up after the pandemic outbreak. However, in the medium term, as we move along the fiscal glide path, buoyancy in revenues, aggressive asset monetisation, efficiency gains, and privatisation would help pay down the public debt, thus bringing down interest payments and releasing more monies for other priorities.

Cooperative fiscal federalism drives a well-targeted fiscal policy

- **Transfer from Centre to States:** Total transfers to States have risen between FY19 and FY23 (BE).

TABLE 3: Trends in Non-tax Revenue of Union Government

	FY18	FY19	FY20	FY21	FY22 PA	FY23 BE	Apr-Nov 2022
							₹ lakh crore
Interest receipts	0.14	0.12	0.12	0.17	0.22	0.18	0.17
Dividends & Profits	0.91	1.13	1.86	0.97	1.61	1.14	0.68
External Grants	0.04	0.01	0.00	0.02	0.01	0.01	0.01
Others	0.84	1.07	1.27	0.90	1.64	1.34	1.12
Non-tax Revenue	1.93	2.36	3.27	2.08	3.48	2.70	1.98
Source: Union Budget Documents, O/o CGA							

- The details of the grants released during the current year.

TABLE 4: Allocation of Grants to the State Governments as Recommended by the 15th FC

No.	Components	Allocation FY23	Amount released (as on 22 November 2022)
			(in ₹ crore)
1	Post Devolution Revenue Deficit Grant	86,201	57,467
2	Disaster Management Grand (Union Share)	23,294	10,976
3	Local Bodies Grants	69,421	28,609
4.	Health Sector Grants	13,192	275
	Grand Total	**1,92,108**	**1,61,230**
Source: Department of Expenditure			

Initiatives by the State Governments to improve their own resources

RBI pointed out that India's property tax collection was much lower than the OECD countries. The Union Government created a scope for a large-scale reform of property taxation practices in India. States like Tamil Nadu, Telangana and Kerala have revised the property taxes in their States during the year to support their revenues. Some states like Tamil Nadu, Andhra Pradesh, Telangana, Karnataka, Madhya Pradesh, Haryana, Kerala, Assam, and UT of Puducherry have considered revising their power tariffs during FY23. In addition, many States have also made efforts towards privatising SPSEs and Monetising assets in FY21 & FY22 to receive additional incentives from the Union Government.

Debt Profile of the Government: IMF projects the global government debt at 91 per cent of GDP in 2022, about 7.5 percentage points above the pre-pandemic levels. Some European economies are expanding their budgets to provide relief to households and small businesses from mounting energy bills.

- **Total liabilities:** The total liabilities of Indian Government was stable before pandemic spiked in FY21. Total liabilities of the Union Government moderated from 59.2 per cent of GDP in FY21 to 56.7 per cent in FY22.
- **Sovereign external debt:** Of the Union Government's total net liabilities in end-March 2021, 95.1 per cent were denominated in domestic currency, while sovereign external debt constituted 4.9 per cent, implying low currency risk.
- **Dated securities:** Over the last few years, the proportion of dated securities maturing in less than five years has declined, whereas long-term securities have shown an increasing trend.
- **Consolidating General government finances:** The General Government liabilities as a proportion of GDP increased steeply during FY21 on account of the additional borrowings made by Centre and States on account of the pandemic. The General Government deficits as a per cent of GDP have also consolidated after their peak in F21.
- **A positive growth-interest rate differential keeps the Government Debt sustainable:** The General Government Debt to GDP ratio increased from 75.7 per cent of end-March 2020 to 89.6 per cent at the end of the pandemic year FY21. It is estimated to decline to 84.5 per cent of GDP by end-March 2022. The emphasis on capex-led growth will enable India to keep the growth-interest rate differential positive. A positive growth-interest rate differential keeps the debt levels sustainable.
- **Government debt to GDP ratio from 2005 to 2021**: For India, this increase is modest, from 81 per cent of GDP in 2005 to around 84 per cent of GDP in 2021. It has been possible on the back of resilient economic growth during the last 15 years leading to a positive growth-interest rate differential, which, in turn, has resulted in sustainable Government debt to GDP levels.

4. MONETARY MANAGEMENT AND FINANCIAL INTERMEDIATION: A GOOD YEAR

Introduction:

The chapter highlights the government's monetary policies and financial management through monetary policies during Covid-19 period, liquidity conditions of different economic sectors, the monetary policy transmissions and role of banks in credit issuing, credit growth in India, NBFC's and their post Covid-19 performance, role of insolvency and bankruptcy code in easy resolvency of Start-up's in India, importance of IFSC-GIFT CITY and development of international financial market in India, Insurance sector and its importance in various sectors and importance of pension sector in India and its coverage.

Monetary developments:

- The conflict in Europe resulted in commodity prices soaring and added significantly to the prevailing inflationary pressures. This development has triggered the current sharp and synchronous monetary tightening cycle. The Monetary Policy Committee (MPC) maintained a tight rope walk on the **policy repo rate.**
- Growth in **Currency in Circulation (CIC)** broadly remained stable at levels seen after Covid-19, barring a marginal increase in the immediate aftermath of the outbreak of the Russia-Ukraine conflict, which can be attributed to a rise in precautionary holdings.
- **The money multiplier** – the ratio of M3 and M0 – has broadly remained stable at an average of 5.1 over April-December 2022 period compared to 5.2 in the corresponding period of the previous year.

Liquidity Conditions

- The **Liquidity Adjustment Facility (LAF)** corridor became symmetric around the policy repo rate.
- **Liquidity management by RBI**: The Reserve Bank remained nimble and agile in liquidity management by conducting two-way operations.

- It injected liquidity to assuage transient liquidity tightness through two **variable rate repo (VRR)** auctions of ₹50,000 crore each of 3 days and overnight maturity on 26th July and 22nd September 2022, respectively. The gradual withdrawal of surplus liquidity pushed the weighted average call rate (WACR) – the operating target of monetary policy – closer to the policy repo rate, on an average basis.

Monetary Policy Transmission

- An analysis of transmission across bank groups during FY23 (up to November 2022) indicates that the increase in the **weighted average lending rate (WALRs)** on fresh loans was higher in the case of public sector banks, while that of the **Weighted Average Domestic Term Deposit Rate (WADTDR)** on outstanding deposits and WALR on outstanding loans was higher for private banks.

Banking Sector

- **Resilient and well-capitalised Banking System:** The asset quality of SCBs has been improving steadily over the years across all major sectors, while **Net Non-Performing Assets (NNPA)** have dropped to a ten-year low of 1.3 per cent of total assets.
- Lower slippages and the reduction in outstanding GNPAs through recoveries, upgrades and write-offs led to this decrease. Lower GNPAs, combined with high provisions accumulated in recent years, contributed to a decline in NNPA.
- The profitability of SCBs, measured in terms of Return on Equity (ROE) and Return on Assets (ROA), improved to levels last observed in FY15. At the system level, Profit After Tax (PAT) witnessed a double-digit growth led by strong growth in Net Interest Income (NII) and a significant lowering of provisions.

Credit Growth Aided by a Sound Banking System and Deleveraged Corporate Sector

- **Credit to agriculture and allied activities** gained momentum supported by the Government's concessional institutional credit and higher agricultural credit target. **Industrial credit growth** has been buoyed by a pick-up in credit to MSMEs, assisted by the benefits accrued from the effective implementation of the **Emergency Credit Line Guarantee Scheme (ECLGS)** and the support provided by the government's **production-linked incentive scheme** and improvement in **capacity utilisation**.

Non-Banking Financial Companies (NBFCs) Continue to Recover

- The continuous **improvement in asset quality** is seen in the declining GNPA ratio of NBFCs reaching close to the pre-pandemic level.
- With the decline in GNPAs, the **capital position of NBFCs also remains robust**, however, it remains well above the regulatory requirement.
- **Credit extended by NBFCs is picking up momentum**, NBFCs continued to deploy the largest quantum of credit from their balance sheets to the industrial sector, followed by retail, services, and agriculture.

Progress made under the Insolvency and Bankruptcy Code

- **Ease of doing business: Facilitating the process of 'exit':** Since the inception of the IBC **Corporate Insolvency Resolution Processes (CIRPs)** large number of cases have been closed. The Code also provides for a **Corporate Debtor (CD)** to **voluntarily liquidate** itself subject to the fulfilment of certain conditions as prescribed under the Code.

Development in Capital Markets: Global macroeconomic uncertainty, unprecedented inflation, monetary policy tightening, volatile markets, etc., resulted in hurting investor sentiments.

Primary Market

- **Equity: Large number of SMEs coming out with the public offer:** From the buoyant performance of the primary market has been observed despite turmoil in global financial markets.

- **Debt: Underactivity in public debt issuances more than compensated by private debt placements:** The amount of resources mobilised by the issuance of debt securities in the primary market increased. The total number of issues in the same period also increased by the underactivity in public debt issuances was more than compensated by private debt placements. The number of private debt placements increased by 11 per cent from 851 to 945, while resources mobilised increased by 6 per cent in April-November 2022, compared to the corresponding period in the year before.

Strong macroeconomic fundamentals ensure India remains an attractive destination:

- Global economic factors, such as inflationary pressures, monetary tightening by central banks and recessionary fears in Advanced Economies, exerted pressure on FPIs to sell in Indian markets.
- Investments by **Domestic Institutional Investors (DIIs)** acted as a countervailing force against FPI outflows during recent years, rendering the Indian equity market relatively less susceptible to large scale corrections. Net DII inflows and net investment by mutual funds in equities were observed during FY23 (until November 2022).

IFSC – GIFT City

Setting up and operationalising India's maiden International Financial Services Centre (IFSC) in GIFT City is the most important one. The aim is to facilitate India to emerge as a significant economic power by accelerating the development of a strong base of International Financial Services in the country.

GIFT IFSC - Emerging as a Preferred Jurisdiction for International Financial Services

GIFT IFSC has more than 390 + entities registered across a full spectrum of financial services, including Banks, Capital Markets, Insurance, FinTech, Aircraft Leasing, Bullion Exchange, etc. The financial services market is rapidly growing with the healthy and increasing participation of international and domestic financial institutions. The significance of GIFT IFSC can be viewed as:

- Recent developments/milestones/innovations/collaborations with other countries.
- Multilateral Memorandum of Understanding (MMoU)
- Bilateral Memorandum of Understanding (BMoU)
- FinTech bridge with the Monetary Authority of Singapore
- NSE IFSC-SGX Connect
- Visibility and Mindshare Among FinTechs globally
- Cooperation agreement between India INX and Luxembourg Stock Exchange
- IFSCA Vision for FY24 and beyond

Developments in the Insurance Market

- **Insurance markets globally have demonstrated remarkable flexibility and resilience in overcoming the impact of the pandemic:** Internationally, the potential and performance of the insurance sector are generally assessed based on two parameters, viz., **'insurance penetration',** which refers to the ratio of total insurance premiums to Gross Domestic Product (GDP) in a year and **'insurance density'**, which refers to the ratio of insurance premium to population, i.e.; insurance premium per capita and is measured in US Dollar, as they reflect the level of development of the insurance sector in a country.
- **India poised to emerge as one of the fastest-growing insurance markets in the coming decade:** Insurance penetration in India increased steadily. Life insurance penetration in India was 3.2 per cent in 2021, almost twice more than the emerging markets and slightly above the global average. However, most life insurance products sold in India are savings-linked, with just a small protection component.
- To facilitate the penetration of insurance to the lower income segments of the population, the Insurance Regulatory and Development Authority of India (IRDAI) issued IRDAI (Micro Insurance) Regulations, 2015, which provide a platform for distributing insurance products that are affordable for the rural and urban poor and promote financial inclusion.

- The government's flagship initiative for crop insurance**, Pradhan Mantri Fasal Bima Yojana (PMFBY)**, has led to significant growth in the premium income for crop insurance. **Ayushman Bharat (Pradhan Mantri Jan Arogya Yojana) (AB PMJAY)** aims at providing a health cover of ₹5 lakh per family per year for secondary and tertiary care hospitalisation.
- As per **the Swiss Re Institute World Insurance: 'Inflation risks front and centre report**, India is one of the fastest-growing insurance markets in the world in total premium volumes.

Pension Sector

- **India's Pension Sector demonstrated remarkable performance during the Covid-19:** The Government of India announced various measures to provide pensions to families who have lost their earning members due to Covid. It also took initiatives towards enhancing and liberalising insurance compensation. The benefit of the **Employees State Insurance Corporation (ESIC)** pension scheme was extended to even those who have lost earning members due to Covid-19. The insurance benefits under the **Employees Deposit Linked Insurance (EDLI) scheme** were also enhanced and liberalised.
- To enhance the **"Ease of Living"** of Central Government Civil Pensioners, **an Electronic Pension Payment order (e-PPO)** was integrated with Digi Locker, creating a permanent PPO record in the Digi Locker.
- The Government of India is implementing various pension schemes such as the **Indira Gandhi National Old Age Pension Scheme (IGNOAPS), Indira Gandhi National Widow Pension Scheme (IGNWPS)**, Indira Gandhi National Disability Pension Scheme (IGNDPS) under the **National Social Assistance Programme (NSAP)** with a total beneficiary coverage of 4.7 crore.
- The **National Pension System (NPS)** was introduced in January 2004, the primary pension system for government employees with a pay-as-you-go defined benefit plan. NPS for government employees is a defined contribution plan with co-contribution from the government.

- **The Government introduced APY in June 2015** as a part of the overarching objective of providing universal social security. The scheme applies to all individuals aged 18-40 years, with an emphasis on underprivileged, unorganised, and low-income individuals.
- PFRDA, under the aegis of the **Financial Stability and Development Council (FSDC),** has taken several steps to enhance financial education so that consumers can make informed decisions and reap the benefit of the formal financial sector while being cognizant of risks and various trade-offs involved. These include pension education through print and electronic media, outreach programs through trade bodies, intermediaries such as banks, and town hall events.

Outlook

- The resilience of the domestic financial system is reflected in the healthy balance sheet of banks, stronger capital levels of NBFCs and robust growth in the AUM of domestic mutual funds. Buoyant demand for bank credit and early signs of a revival in the investment cycle are benefiting from improving asset quality, a return to profitability and resilient capital and liquidity buffers.
- India is one of the fastest-growing insurance markets in the world and is expected to emerge as one of the top six insurance markets by 2032.
- Digitisation of India's insurance market, accompanied by an increase in FDI limit for insurance companies, is likely to facilitate an increased flow of long-term capital, a global technology, processes, and international best practices, which will support the growth of India's insurance sector.

5. PRICES AND INFLATION: SUCCESSFUL TIGHT-ROPE WALKING

Introduction (Phases of Inflation)

- **A trend of rising phase up to April 2022 when it crested at 7.8 per cent** due to the fallout of the Russia-Ukraine war and a shortfall in crop harvests due to excessive heat in some parts of the country.

- **A decline to around 5.7 per cent by December 2022:** Global economic slowdown and interest rate increases brought down commodity prices, contributing to a substantial decline in wholesale price inflation. Thus, input price pressures on Indian manufacturers abated.

Core inflation remains sticky and reflects the second-round effects of the supply shocks witnessed earlier this year. Further, with the recovery of demand, there has been a pickup in service inflation.

Domestic Retail Inflation:

- Lower CPI-Combined (CPI-C) based retail inflation.
- Some sub-groups such as 'oils & fats', 'fuel & light' and 'transport & communication' reported high inflation. There are two reasons behind this supply disruptions caused by pandemic and headline inflation caused by Russia-Ukraine crisis.
- Retail inflation trend was mainly driven by higher food inflation, while core inflation stayed at a moderate level.
- Food inflation ranged between 4.2 per cent to 8.6 per cent

Retail Inflation Driven by Food Commodities:

- Retail price inflation mainly stems from the agriculture and allied sector, housing, textiles, and pharmaceutical sectors.
- 'Food & beverages', 'clothing & footwear', and 'fuel & light' were the major contributors to headline inflation– the first two contributing more this fiscal than in the previous one

Some initiative to combat food inflation

- The Central Government, imposed an export duty of 20 per cent on rice, brown rice, and semi-milled as well as wholly milled rice, except parboiled rice.

- The Central Government, decided to provide 1.5 million tonnes of Chana to States and UTs at a discounted rate for distribution under various welfare schemes. The states will be able to procure Chana at a discount of ₹8 per kg over their respective issue prices.
- Central Government directed leading Edible Oil Associations to ensure a reduction in the maximum retail price of edible oils by ₹15 per litre with immediate effect.

Rural-Urban Inflation Differential has Declined:

- Rural inflation has remained above its urban counterpart throughout the current fiscal year, reversing the trend seen during the pandemic years.

Measures to Contain Inflation in Input Prices

- **Fuel Prices:** The Central Government has made interventions by calibrating the excise duties on petrol and diesel.
- **Plastic products:** The import duty on import of raw materials used in the plastic industry has been reduced to lower the cost of domestic manufacturing.
- **Steel:** Import duty on major inputs – ferronickel, cooking coal, PCI coal – has been cut from 2.5 per cent to zero, while the duty on coke and semi-coke has been slashed from 5 per cent to zero.
- **Cotton:** The government waived customs duty on cotton imports until 30 September 2022, to benefit the textile industry and lower prices for consumers.
- **Diamonds and gemstones:** Customs duty on cut and polished diamonds and gemstones was reduced to 5 per cent and duty on the simply sawn diamond was reduced to nil.
- **Chemical products:** Customs duty on certain critical chemicals namely methanol, acetic acid and heavy feedstocks for petroleum refining was reduced.

Convergence of WPI and CPI Inflation

The convergence between the WPI and CPI indices was mainly driven by two factors:

- Firstly, a cooling in inflation of commodities such as crude oil, iron, aluminium and cotton led to a lower WPI.
- Secondly, CPI inflation rose due to an increase in the prices of services. Services form a part of the core component of the CPI-C but are not included in the WPI basket.

Falling Inflationary Expectations:

- Businesses and household inflation expectations too have moderated.

How is the Current Inflation Different from the 1970s?

- Recent oil price rises are proportionally smaller. Commodity supply disruptions have played a smaller role in recent price increases, central banks have much clearer and more robust institutional frameworks that focus on price stability today.
- However, in 1973 crisis closely followed the collapse of the Bretton Woods managed exchange rate regime as the goals and even instruments of monetary policy were poorly defined in many countries.

Housing Prices: Recovering Housing Sector after the Pandemic:

- Monitoring housing prices is essential for achieving the objectives of price stability, financial stability, and growth.
- The National Housing Bank (NHB) publishes two Housing Price Indices (HPI), namely 'HPI assessment price' and 'HPI market price quarterly', with FY18 as the base year. Out of the 50 cities, 43 saw an increase in the index, whereas 7 cities showed a decline annually. Metros city also showed improvement.

Pharmaceutical sectors:

- **National List of Essential Medicines (NLEM-2015)**, NLEM 2022 was promulgated by Ministry of Health and Family Welfare in September 2022 and revised Schedule I of Drugs (Prices Control) Order (DPCO) was notified on 11 November 2022 by Department of Pharmaceuticals incorporating NLEM, 2022.

- **Pradhan Mantri Bhartiya Janaushadhi Pariyojana (PMBJP)** was launched to make quality generic medicines available at affordable prices to all.

Broad Observation

- Both CPI-C and WPI have fallen below 6 per cent.
- International crude oil prices, the principal drivers of inflation this financial year, have returned to normal levels.
- The re-emergence of Covid-19 in China can trigger supply chain disruptions as was the case during the pandemic period.
- The geopolitics associated with oil can particularly affect our imported inflation.
- RBI forecasts elevated domestic prices for cereals and spices in the near term owing to supply shortages. RBI forecasts elevated domestic prices for cereals and spices in the near term owing to supply shortages.
- Next year, it is expected, monetary and fiscal authorities to be as proactive and vigilant as they have been this year.

6. SOCIAL INFRASTRUCTURE AND EMPLOYMENT

Introduction

- **Quality employment opportunities and working conditions** are the essential instruments to chisel this potential into long-term sustainable growth. **In its Amrit Kaal** for the next 25 years, India envisions rewarding itself with the dividends that can come from demographics.
- Clean drinking water, sanitation, employment prospects, health care, social security, connectivity, etc. all these together determine the quality of life.
- In the Financial Year 2023, various dimensions of the sector are recouping lost grounds and are on the path of reenergising to meet the vision of "sabka sath, sabka vikas and sabka vishwas".

Social Sector Expenditure

- Social Sector Expenditure keeping pace with growing importance of the sector.
- The share of expenditure on social services in the total expenditure of the Government has increased to 26.6 per cent in FY23 (BE).
- The share of expenditure on health in the total expenditure on social services, has increased.
- Fifteenth Finance Commission, in its report, had recommended that public health expenditure of Union and States together should be increased in a progressive manner to reach 2.5 per cent of GDP by 2025.

Improving Human Development Parameter:

- 'Human Development' is the key enabler for upward social mobility.
- According to United Nations Development Programme (UNDP) report, 90 per cent of countries have registered a reduction in their Human Development Index (HDI) indicating that human development across the world has stalled for the first time in 32 years.
- India ranked 132 out of 191 countries and territories on the 2021/2022 HDI report.
- On the parameter of **gender inequality,** India's Gender Inequality Index (GII) value is 0.490 in 2021 and is ranked 122. This score is better than that of the South Asian region.

Transformation of Aspirational Districts Programme

- The Government of India launched the 'Transformation of Aspirational Districts' (Aspirational Districts Programme (ADP)) initiative in January 2018 with a vision of a New India by 2022.
- 117 Aspirational Districts (ADs) across 28 States/UTs have been identified by NITI Aayog based upon composite indicators.
- The broad contours of the programme are Convergence (of Central & State Schemes), Collaboration (of Central, State level Nodal Officers & District Collectors), and Competition among districts through monthly delta ranking; all driven by a mass movement.

Achievements of this program:

- Many aspirational districts have surpassed the average state values in several indicators under the Health and Nutrition theme monitored under the programme. For instance, in 10 indicators of health, 73 ADs have surpassed the state averages.
- All districts have made significant improvements across different indicators. For instance, under Health and Nutrition, 46 districts have improved by up to 45 per cent.
- While monitoring the outcome of financial inclusion, it was seen that aspirational district have performed better than non-aspirational districts.
- Several aspirational district ADs have reported saturation in the basic infrastructure indicators like percentage of households with electricity connection; percentage of habitations with access to all-weather roads.

Template of good Governance: At present, two programmes have been conceptualised along the lines of ADP design, one is 'Mission Utkarsh' and the other is 'Aspirational Blocks Programme' (ABP).

Labour Reforms:

- Efficient labour codes and use of technology, such as web-based Inspection has been introduced in order to ensure transparency and accountability in enforcement. Decriminalisation of minor offences has also been provided in the Labour Codes.

Codes related to Labour Reforms:

- Code on Wages, 2019
- The Industrial Relations Code, 2020
- The Code on Social Security, 2020
- Occupational Safety, Health & Working Conditions Code, 2020

- **e-Shram portal:** Ministry of Labour and Employment (MoLE) has developed e-Shram portal for creating a National database of unorganised workers, which is verified with Aadhaar.

- It captures details of workers like name, occupation, address, occupation type, educational qualification, and skill types etc., for the optimum realisation of their employability and extend the benefits of the social security schemes to them.
- It is the first-ever national database of unorganised workers, including migrant workers, construction workers, gig and platform workers, etc.
- Currently, e-Shram portal has been linked to NCS portal and ASEEM portal for seamless facilitation of services.

Aadhaar: The Many Achievements of the Unique Identity

- **Aadhaar – Usage in DBT:** The number is sufficient to transfer any payment to an individual's bank account through Aadhaar Payment Bridge (APB), .
- **Aadhaar Enabled Payment Systems (AEPS):** This has immensely facilitated providing door-step banking services and helped mitigate the hardships of the people due to the Covid-19 pandemic.
- **JAM (Jan-Dhan, Aadhaar, and Mobile)** trinity, combined with the power of DBT, has brought the marginalised sections of society into the formal financial system.
- **One Nation One Ration Card (ONORC) Scheme:** Free distribution of food grains under 'Pradhan Mantri Garib Kalyan Yojana' (PMGKY) has greatly mitigated the Covid pandemic's impact.
- **PM Kisan Samman Nidhi:** It is an initiative by the Government of India that give farmers upto ₹6,000 per year as minimum income support.

Major issue in female labor force participation rate:

- The common narrative of Indian women's low LFPR misses the reality of working females integral to the economy of the household and the country. Measurement of employment through the survey design and content can make a significant difference to final LFPR estimates, and this matters more for measuring female LFPR than male LFPR.
- No recovery questions in the PLFS questionnaire.

Role of Self-Help Groups in Women's Empowerment

- India has around 1.2 crore SHGs, 88 per cent being all-women SHGs. Success stories include Kudumbashree in Kerala, Jeevika in Bihar, Mahila Arthik Vikas Mahila Mandal in Maharashtra, and recently, Looms of Ladakh.
- **Impact of SHGs: Empowered Women, Empowered Hinterland-** Women's economic SHGs have a positive, statistically significant effect on women's economic, social, and political empowerment, with positive effects on empowerment achieved through various pathways.

Quarterly Employment Survey (QES)

The QES, **conducted by the Labour Bureau**, covers establishments with 10 or more workers in nine major sectors viz. manufacturing, construction, trade, transport, education, health, accommodation & restaurants, IT/BPOs, and financial services.

- The Annual Survey of Industries (ASI), conducted by **MoSPI**, is an important source of industrial statistics of the registered organised manufacturing sector of the economy. It covers all factories registered of the **Factories Act, 1948**, i.e., those factories employing 10 or more workers using power; and those employing 20 or more workers without using power.

Formal Employment:

- **Aatmanirbhar Bharat Rojgar Yojana (ABRY), launched in October 2020:** Total registration under the scheme is 75.1 lakh, and total benefits of ₹8,210 crore have been given to 60.2 lakh beneficiaries through 1.5 lakh establishments till now.
- **Demand for work under MGNREGS:** The number of persons demanding work under MGNREGS was seen to be trending around pre-pandemic levels.

National Career Service Project

The 'National Career Service (NCS') project was launched in July 2015, as a one-stop solution providing an array of employment and career-related services. It works towards bridging the gap between candidates and employers; candidates seeking training and career guidance and agencies providing training and career counselling.

The trend in rural wages:

- Nominal rural wages have increased at a steady positive rate during FY23.
- However, growth in real rural wages has been negative due to elevated inflation.

Ensuring Quality Education for All

- NEP 2020 was laid down as the first education policy of the 21st century, aiming to address the many growing developmental imperatives of the country.
- Samagra Shiksha in 2018 as an overarching programme for the school education sector extending from pre-school to class XII with an aim to ensure inclusive and equitable quality education at all levels of school education.

School Enrolment

- The year FY22 saw improvement in Gross Enrolment Ratios (GER) in schools and improvement in gender parity. GER in the primary enrolment in class I to V as a percentage of the population in age 6 to 10 years for girls as well as boys have improved.

School Drop-out

- School drop-out rates at all levels have witnessed a steady decline in recent years. The decline is for both girls and boys.

School Infrastructure

- The education infrastructure in the form of schools, amenities, and digitalisation has been steadily promoted along with a focus on pedagogy.
- Further, the availability of teachers, measured by pupil-teacher ratio, an indicator which is inversely related to improvement in quality of education, has improved at all levels.

PM Schools for Rising India: These schools will be equipped with modern infrastructure and showcase the implementation of the NEP and emerge as exemplary schools over a period of time, while offering leadership to other schools in the neighbourhood.

The National Curriculum Framework (NCF) for Foundational Stage: NCF for Foundational Stage has been launched as the new 5+3+3+4 curricular structure which integrates early childhood care and education for all children of ages 3 to 8.

- **Pilot project of Balvatika:** With a focus which is meant to prepare children with cognitive affective, and psychomotor abilities and also early literacy and numeracy for students in the age groups of 3+, 4+ and 5+ years to read, write & develop number sense through a play-based approach.
- **Toy-based pedagogy:** A handbook for Toy-based pedagogy has been designed to promote the integration of indigenous toys and their pedagogy into the curriculum of school education, early childhood care and education and teacher education.
- **Screening tools (Mobile App) for specific learning disabilities**: PRASHAST, a Disability Screening mobile app, has been launched, covering 21 disabilities, including the benchmark disabilities as per the Rights of Persons with Disabilities Act 2016.
- **National Credit Framework (NCrF):** Taking the vision of the new NEP, the NCrF is an umbrella framework for skilling, re-skilling, up-skilling, accreditation and evaluation, seamlessly integrating the credits earned through school education, higher education, and vocational and skill education by encompassing the National Higher Education Qualification Framework (NHEQF), National Skills

Qualification Framework (NSQF) and National School Education Qualification Framework (NSEQF).

- **Strengthening Teaching-Learning and Results for States (STARS):** STARS Project is being implemented as a CSS in six states namely Himachal Pradesh, Madhya Pradesh, Rajasthan, Maharashtra, Odisha and Kerala over a period of 5 years.
- **Vidyanjali (A School Volunteer Initiative):** With the aim of strengthening schools and improving the quality of school education through community, Corporate Social Responsibility (CSR) and private sector involvement across the country.
- **Samagra Shiksha Scheme:** A CSS of Samagra Shiksha of the Department of School Education and Literacy is an overarching programme for the school education sector extending from pre-school to class XII.

Higher Education:

Initiatives for higher education

- **Research & Development Cell (RDC) in Higher Education Institutions (HEI):** The University Grants Commission (UGC) launched an initiative to establish an RDC in HEIs with the mandate for promoting quality research that contributes meaningfully towards the goal of a self-reliant India, aligned with the provisions of NEP 2020.

Akhil Bharatiya Shiksha Samagam

A three-day Akhil Bharatiya Shiksha Samagam was organised at Varanasi on 7-9 July 2022 by the Ministry of Education in association with the UGC and Banaras Hindu University.

Equipping the Workforce with Employable Skills and Knowledge in Mission Mode:

- Skill development is aimed at the removal of the disconnect between demand and supply of skilled manpower, building vocational and technical training framework, skill up-gradation, and building of new skills, and innovative thinking not only for existing jobs but also jobs of the future.

Skill India Mission

- Under the Mission, the government, through more than 20 Central Ministries/Departments, is implementing various skill development schemes across the country.
- **Quality and Affordable Health for All**
- Under the National Health Mission, the Government has made concerted efforts to engage with all relevant sectors and stakeholders to move in the direction of achieving universal health coverage and delivering quality healthcare services to all at affordable cost.

Health Expenditure Estimates

- The social security expenditure on health, which includes the social health insurance programme, government-financed health insurance schemes, and medical reimbursements made to government employees, has increased from 6 per cent in FY14 to 9.6 per cent in FY19.

Rural health care – strengthening of infrastructure and human resource

FIGURE 5: Rural Health Care System in India

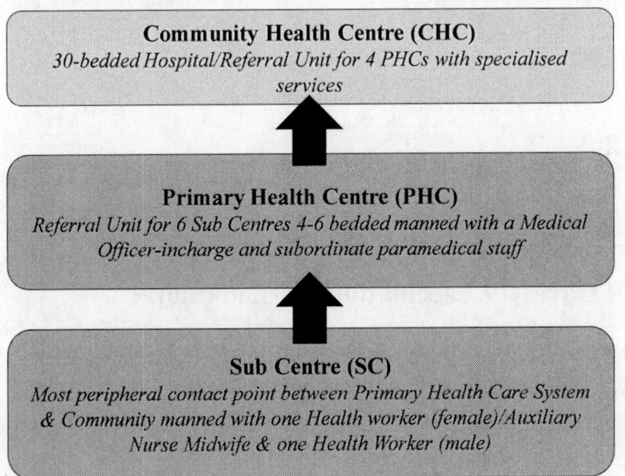

Progress under Major Government Initiatives for Health

eSanjeevani:

eSanjeevani is an innovative, indigenous, cost-effective, and integrated cloud-based telemedicine system application to enable patient-to-doctor teleconsultation to ensure a continuum of care and facilitate health services to all citizens in the confines of their homes, free of cost.

- **Progress under Ayushman Bharat:** Approximately 22 crore beneficiaries have been verified under the Scheme including 3 crore beneficiaries.
- **Deworming: a low-cost high-returns intervention**

Figure 6: Channels of the Impact of Deworming

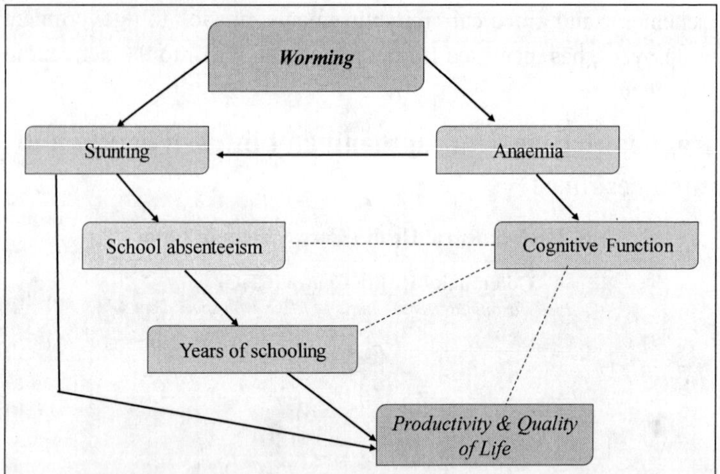

National Covid-19 Vaccination Programme:

- India's National Covid-19 Vaccination Programme, which is the world's largest vaccination programme, began on 16 January 2021, initially with the aim of covering the adult population of the country in the shortest possible time.

Social Protection for the Rainy Day

- Pradhan Mantri Vaya Vandana Yojana (PMVVY), Pradhan Mantri Jeevan Jyoti Bima Yojana (PMJJY), PM Street Vendor's Atmanirbhar Nidhi Scheme (PM SVANidhi) etc.
- **Development of India's Aspiring Rural Economy:** It presently stands at 65 per cent for 2021. Further, 47 per cent of the population is dependent on agriculture for livelihood. Thus, the focus of the government on rural development is imperative.

FIGURE 7: Multifaceted Initiatives to Improve the Ecosystem of Quality of Life

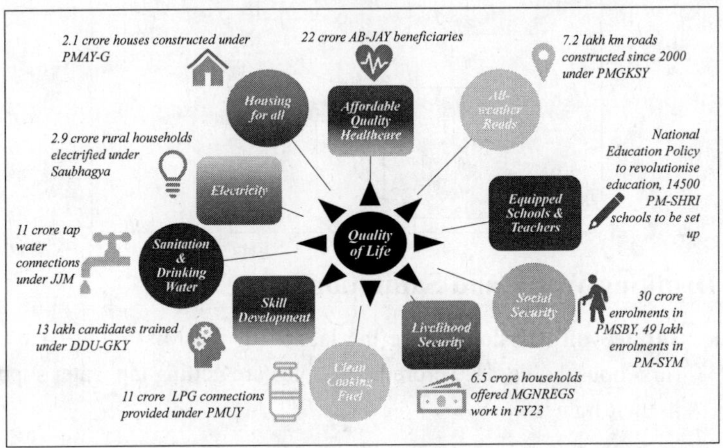

Enhancing Rural Incomes: Deendayal Antyodaya Yojana-National Rural Livelihood Mission (DAY-NRLM) - The cornerstone of the Mission is its 'community-driven' approach which has provided a huge platform in the form of community institutions for women empowerment. Rural women are at the core of the programme.

Deen Dayal Upadhyaya Grameen Kaushalya Yojana (DDU-GKY):

- DDU-GKY is a placement-linked skill development programme for rural poor youth under the NRLM.

- **Rural Housing:** Providing around 3 crore pucca houses with basic amenities to all eligible houseless households living in kutcha and dilapidated houses in rural areas by 2024.

FIGURE 8: Components of DAY-NRLM

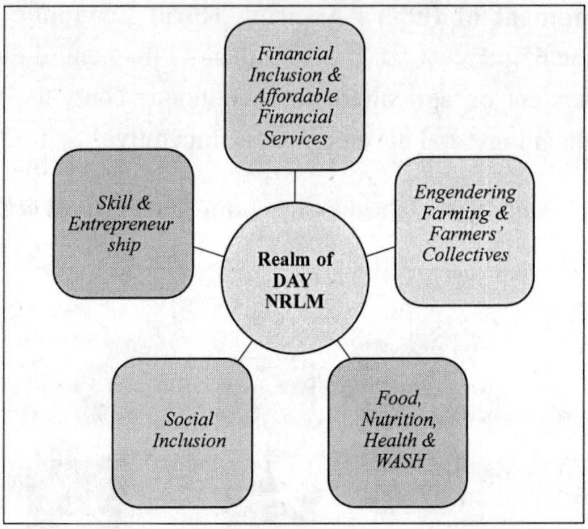

Drinking Water and Sanitation:

- **Jal Jeevan Mission:** Since the launch of the Mission, 19.4 crore rural households, 11.0 crore households are getting tap water supply in their homes.
- **Gram Panchayats,** and more than 1.5 lakh villages have also become **'Har Ghar Jal Block'**, **'Har Ghar Jal Panchayat'**, and **'Har Ghar Jal Gaon'** respectively.
- **Jal Jeevan Mission as an instrument of public health:** With the availability of safe and potable drinking water at the doorstep of every rural household, water-borne diseases have drastically reduced.

Mission Amrit Sarovar was launched on National Panchayati Raj Day on 24 April 2022 with the objective to conserve water for the future. The Mission is aimed at developing and rejuvenating 75 water bodies in each district of the country during this Amrit Varsh, 75th Years of Independence.

- **JALDOOT App:** JALDOOT App was launched on 27 September 2022 for measuring the water level in a Gram Panchayat through 2-3 selected open wells twice a year (pre-monsoon and post monsoon).
- **LPG CONNECTION:**
    - Under this Ujjwala 2.0 scheme, 1.6 crore connections have been released until 24 November 2022.
- **Rural connectivity: Pradhan Mantri Gram Sadak Yojana:** Since its inception, a total of 1,84,984 roads measuring 8,01,838 km and 10,383 Long Span Bridges (LSBs) have been sanctioned under all the interventions/verticals of PMGSY.

Electricity:

- The **Saubhagya scheme** has been successfully completed and closed on 31 March 2022.
- **Deendayal Upadhyaya Gram Jyoti Yojana (DDUGJY):** A total of 2.9 crore households have been electrified since the launch of the Saubhagya period in October 2017 under various schemes viz. (Saubhagya, DDUGJY, etc.).

Direct Benefit Transfer: A Game Changer

- Since the inception of DBT, cumulative transfers of over ₹26.5 lakh crore in respect of Central schemes have been made through the DBT route.

Enhancing Rural Governance for Inclusive Growth

- Rashtriya Gram Swaraj Abhiyan - The scheme has been revamped and approved in April 2022 for implementation over the period FY23 to FY26. The focus of the scheme of Revamped RGSA is on re-imagining PRIs as vibrant centres of local self-governance with a special focus on the Localisation of SDGs (LSDGs) at the grassroots level.

Conclusion

With the vision of 'Minimum Government; Maximum Governance', further developments will hold the key to attaining more equitable economic growth. Evident ones include stepping up learning outcomes through digital and teaching interventions in schools, enhancing the role of community workers in healthcare, pushing SHGs through better product design and up scaling enterprises.

7. CLIMATE CHANGE & ENVIRONMENT: PREPARING TO FACE THE FUTURE

This chapter presents an updated discussion on the issue of climate change from India's perspective, including a discussion on forests and their role in mitigating carbon emissions, an approach to transition to renewable energy and the recently submitted low emissions development strategy.

- India has integrated the development goals with ambitious climate action goals, be it in the form of augmented solar power capacity, higher energy saving targeting notified in **PAT cycle-VII**, improved green cover facilitated by **Green India Mission**, among other targeted Government actions.
- **Financial constraints:** The availability of adequate and affordable finance remains a constraint in India's climate actions. Finance is a critical input for its climate actions. Therefore, the country has scaled up its efforts towards mobilising private capital, including through sovereign green bonds, to meet climate action goals.
- **GHG emissions** are the most significant threat to humanity and the inescapable reality the world faces. Action to reduce carbon emissions and adapt to the changing climatic conditions are required urgently.
- **Displacement:** It is estimated that by 2030, about 700 million people worldwide will be at risk of displacement by drought alone (U.N. SDG Portal).
- **Hotspots:** The IPCC's Sixth Assessment Report (AR6) notes that high **human vulnerability global hotspots** are found particularly in **West, Central & East Africa, South Asia, Central, and South America, Small Island Developing States, and the Arctic.** Further, as per the report, **Asia** is most vulnerable to climate change, especially to **extreme heat, flooding, sea level rise, and erratic rainfall.**

India's commitments:

- India last updated its **climate pledges** in 2022 of reducing emissions intensity — or the volume of emissions per unit of gross domestic product (GDP) — by 45% from 2005 levels by 2030, a 10% increase from what it agreed to in 2015.
- The government committed to meet **50% of its electric power** needs from renewable, non-fossil fuel energy sources — up from 40% committed at the Paris agreement.
- It assured to create an additional carbon sink of **2.5 to 3 billion tonnes of CO_2-equivalent [$GtCO_2e$]** through additional forest and tree cover by 2030.

India's vulnerability to climate change

- India is considered to be one of the most vulnerable countries given its long coastline, monsoon-dependent agriculture, and large agrarian economy. According to a 2020 Germanwatch study, India is the seventh most vulnerable country to climate extremes.
- **India has contributed only 4 per cent (until 2019) to the cumulative global emissions and its per capita emission is far less than the world average.**

Progress on India's Climate Action

- **National Action Plan on Climate Change (NAPCC)** was launched in 2008. It includes establishing eight National Missions, covering several initiatives and a slew of measures in the area of solar, water, energy efficiency, forests, sustainable habitat, sustainable agriculture, sustaining Himalayan ecosystem, capacity building and research and development (R&D).
- **National Adaptation Fund for Climate Change (NAFCC),** a central sector scheme, was initiated in 2015-16 to support adaptation activities in the States and Union Territories (UTs) of India that are vulnerable to the adverse effects of climate change.

- **Updated NDC:** Demonstrating higher ambition in its climate action, the Government of India submitted its updated NDC in 2022.

Schemes

- Green India Mission (GIM)
- Compensatory Afforestation Fund Management and Planning Authority (CAMPA)
- National Afforestation Programme (NAP)
- Green Highway Policy – 2015
- National Agro-forestry Policy
- Sub-Mission on Agro-forestry (SMAF)

Status of Forest and Tree Cover

- The forest and tree cover in India has shown a gradual and steady trend of increase in the last one and a half decades.
- The country ranks third globally with respect to the net gain in average annual forest area between 2010 and 2020.
- **Carbon Stock in India's Forest and Tree Cover:** The Indian State of Forest Report (ISFR) estimates the carbon stock of forests to be about 7,204 million tonnes in 2019, which is an increase of 79.4 million tonnes of carbon stock as compared to the estimates of the previous assessment for 2017. This translates into carbon emissions sequestrated through forest and tree cover to be 30.1 billion tonnes of CO_2 equivalent.
  - Among the Indian States, **Arunachal Pradesh** has the maximum carbon stock in forests (1023.84 million tonnes), followed by **Madhya Pradesh** (609.25 million tonnes). Jammu & Kashmir is contributing the maximum per-hectare carbon stock of 173.41 tonnes, followed by Himachal Pradesh (167.0 tonnes), Sikkim (166.2 tonnes) and Andaman & Nicobar Islands (162.9 tonnes).

Key-highlights of India State of Forest Report-2021

- Forest and tree cover in the country increased by 2,261 square kilometre since the last assessment in 2019.

- India's total forest and tree cover was 80.9 million hectares, which accounted for 24.62% of the geographical area of the country.
- 17 States and Union Territories had more than 33% of their area under forest cover.
  - Madhya Pradesh had the largest forest cover, followed by Arunachal Pradesh, Chhattisgarh, Odisha and Maharashtra.
- The top five States in terms of forest cover as a percentage of their total geographical area were
  - Mizoram (84.53%)
  - Arunachal Pradesh (79.33%)
  - Meghalaya (76%)
  - Manipur (74.34%)
  - Nagaland (73.90%)
- **India's Target to increase forest cover: National Mission for a Green India (GIM)** is one of the eight Missions under the **National Action Plan on Climate Change.** The target under the Mission is **10 million hectares (Mha)** on forest and non-forest lands for increasing the forest/tree cover and to improve the quality of existing forest.

Preservation of Ecosystems: A Critical Adaptation Action

- India has 75 Ramsar sites covering an area of 13.3 lakh ha, and 49 of these have been added in the last 8 years.
- The Government has taken both regulatory and promotional measures to protect and conserve mangroves. The **National Coastal Mission Programme on 'Conservation and Management of Mangroves and Coral Reefs'** is being implemented.
- Regulatory measures are implemented through **Coastal Regulation Zone (CRZ)** Notification (2019) under the **Environment (Protection) Act, 1986; the Wild Life (Protection) Act, 1972; the Indian Forest Act, 1927; the Biological Diversity Act, 2002;** and rules under these Acts as amended from time to time.

Approach to Transition to Renewable Energy Source

- India is progressively becoming a favoured destination for investment in renewables. As per the Renewables 2022 Global Status Report, during the period 2014 -2021, total investment in renewables stood at US$ 78.1 billion in India. Investment in renewable energy has been close to or higher than US$ 10 billion per year since 2016, except for a dip in 2020 likely due to various Covid-19 restrictions.

Green Hydrogen - A critical source of alternate energy

- With a vision to make India an energy-independent nation, and to de-carbonise critical sectors, the Government approved the **National Green Hydrogen Mission** on January 4, 2023 with an initial outlay of ₹19,744 crore. The Mission will facilitate demand creation, production, utilisation and export of Green Hydrogen and mobilisation of over ₹8 lakh crore of investment by 2030.

Finance for Sustainable Development

- **Green Bonds:** The final **Sovereign Green Bonds** framework of India has been issued. The Framework has been designed to comply with the components and key recommendations of the **International Capital Market Association (ICMA) Green Bond Principles (2021).**
- **Green Climate Fund (GCF)**: GCF is a critical element of the **Paris Agreement**. It is the **world's largest climate fund,** mandated to support developing countries raise and realize their **Nationally Determined Contributions (NDC)** ambitions towards low-emissions, climate-resilient pathways.
- **Green Credits Programme:** It is an effort to create a market-based incentive for different kinds of environment-positive actions, not just for carbon emission reductions.
- **Lifestyle for Environment (LiFE)**: It is a global initiative to fight against climate change through community engagement and lifestyle modification.

- **ECO MARK Labelling: Eco Mark,** also known as **Eco Label,** is a symbol applied to ecologically friendly products complying with the requirements of the **Eco Mark Scheme.** The **Bureau of Indian Standards (BIS)** implements the **Eco Mark Scheme** under the **BIS Act, 1986**.

8. AGRICULTURE & FOOD MANAGEMENT: FROM FOOD SECURITY TO NUTRITIONAL SECURITY

Introduction

- With its solid forward linkages, the agriculture and allied activities sector significantly contributed to the country's overall growth and development by ensuring food security.
  - The Indian agriculture sector has been growing at an average annual growth rate of 4.6 per cent during the last six years. It grew by 3.0 per cent in 2021-22 compared to 3.3 per cent in 2020-21.
  - In 2020-21, exports of agriculture and allied products from India grew by 18 per cent over the previous year.
  - During 2021-22, agricultural exports reached an all-time high of US$ 50.2 billion.
- This period of buoyant performance could be ascribed to the measures taken by the Government to promote **farmer-producer organisations, encourage crop diversification, and improve productivity in agriculture** through support provided for **mechanisation** and the creation of **the Agriculture Infrastructure Fund**.
- Further, income support to farmers through the **Pradhan Mantri Kisan Samman Nidhi (PM-KISAN)** and the promotion of allied activities has led to diversification in sources of farmers' income, improving their resilience to weather shocks.

Government Interventions

- **MSP to Ensure Returns over the Cost of Production:** The Union Budget for 2018-19 announced that farmers in India would be given an MSP of at least one and a half times the cost of production.
- **Enhanced Access to Agricultural Credit:** The **Kisan Credit Card Scheme (KCC)** was introduced in 1998 for farmers to empower them to purchase agricultural products and services on credit at any time. Total number of operative KCC Accounts as on March 2023 are 7.35 crores with total sanctioned limit of ₹ 8.85 lakh crores. To ensure that the farmers pay a minimal interest rate to the banks, the Government of India has introduced **the Interest Subvention Scheme (ISS), now renamed Modified Interest Subvention Scheme** (MISS), to provide **short-term credit** to farmers at subsidised interest rates.
- **Farm mechanization:** Farm mechanisation helps increase productivity through timely and efficient use of other inputs and natural resources while at the same time reducing the cost of cultivation and the drudgery associated with various farm operations.
- **Chemical-free India: Organic and Natural Farming:** India has 44.3 lakh organic farmers, the highest in the world, and about 59.1 lakh ha area was brought under organic farming by 2021-22.
    - Sikkim voluntarily adopted going organic. It became the first state in the world to become fully organic, and other states, including Tripura and Uttarakhand, have set similar targets.
    - The Government has been promoting organic farming by implementing two dedicated schemes, i.e., **Paramparagat Krishi Vikas Yojana (PKVY)** and **Mission Organic Value Chain Development for North Eastern Region (MOVCDNER)** since 2015 through cluster/farmer Producer Organisations (FPOs) formation. PKVY Scheme is being implemented in a cluster mode.

Other Important Initiatives in Agriculture

- PM KISAN Scheme
- Agriculture Infrastructure Fund (AIF)
- Pradhan Mantri Fasal Bima Yojana (PMFBY)
- Mission for Integrated Development of Horticulture (MIDH)
- National Agriculture Market (e-NAM) Scheme

Important Initiatives in Allied Sectors

- The Animal Husbandry Infrastructure Development Fund (AHIDF)
- National Livestock Mission (NLM)
- The Livestock Health and Disease Control (LH&DC) Scheme
- National Animal Disease Control Programme (NADCP)
- Pradhan Mantri Matsya Sampada Yojana (PMMSY)
- Fisheries and Aquaculture Infrastructure Development Fund (FIDF)

Allied Sectors: Animal Husbandry, Dairying and Fisheries Catching Up in Recent Years

- Recognizing the growing importance of allied sectors, the Committee on Doubling Farmers' Income considers dairying, livestock, poultry, fisheries and horticulture as high-growth engines and has recommended a focused policy with a concomitant support system for the allied sector.
- The dairy sector is the most critical component of the livestock sector, employing more than eight crore farmers directly, and is the most prominent agrarian product. Other livestock products, such as eggs and meat, are also growing in importance. While **India ranks first in milk production in the world, it ranks third in egg production and eighth in meat production in the world.**

Food Processing Sector - The Sunrise Sector

- Recognising the abundant potential of the sector, the Government has been at the forefront with various interventions aimed at the development of food processing in the country. The Ministry of Food Processing Industries, through the component schemes of **Pradhan Mantri Kisan SAMPADA Yojana (PMKSY),** provide financial assistance for the overall growth and development of the food processing sector.

- The Ministry also launched in 2020 the **Prime Minister's Formalisation of Micro Food Processing Enterprises (PMFME) Scheme** as part of the ANB Abhiyan to enhance the competitiveness of individual micro-enterprises in the unorganised segment.
- The **Production Linked Incentive Scheme for Food Processing Industry (PLISFPI)**, launched in March 2022, has the specific mandate to incentivise investments to create global food champions. Sectors with high growth potential, like marine products, processed fruits & vegetables, and 'Ready to Eat/ Ready to Cook' products, are covered for support.

Food Security- Social & Legal Commitment to the People of the Nation

- **Food security is not only a question of the ability to produce food but also of the ability to access food.**
- The Government is currently running the most extensive legislation-based food security programme in the world, covering about 80 crore of India's population under **the National Food Security Act (NFSA), 2013.**
- To further ease the process of access to food, the Government launched a citizen-centric and technology-driven scheme in 2019 called the **One Nation One Ration Card (ONORC) scheme.** The ONORC system enables intra-State and inter-State portability of ration cards. It helps the migrant beneficiaries access their food security entitlements from any fair price shop (FPS) of their choice by using the same ration card after biometric/Aadhaar authentication on electronic Point of Sale (e-PoS) devices at the FPS.

9. INDUSTRY: STEADY RECOVERY

Overview of Indian industries

The industry holds a prominent position in the Indian economy contributing about 30 percent of total gross value added in the country.

India has a unique opportunity to become a global manufacturing hub this decade. In this context, the government's **Make-in-India initiative** has facilitated investment, fostered innovation and built world-class infrastructure while addressing the gaps in domestic manufacturing capabilities. The **Production Linked Incentive (PLI) schemes** across 14 categories has further complemented it.

Demand Stimulus to Industrial Growth

- FY23 began with the Russian-Ukraine conflict showing no signs of relenting. As the year ended, the conflict appears to have plateaued, although global commodity prices are yet to de-escalate to their pre-pandemic levels.
- Industry, throughout the year, has thus faced high input costs imported into the country. Fearing demand impact, the industry has been gradually passing on the higher production costs, which has led to sticky but non-rising core retail inflation.
- **Non-core retail inflation**, on the other hand, comprising food and energy components, has been declining as local weather extremities have eased and interventions by the government to restrict price rises have proven effective. The consequent decrease in overall retail inflation has thus sustained the pent-up consumer demand in the post-pandemic Indian economy, inducing an industrial recovery despite the global headwinds.

Supply Response of Industry

- Robust growth in the production of capital goods and infrastructure/ construction goods is indicative of the beginnings of an **investment cycle** in the private sector in the next financial year.
- The eight core industries of **coal, fertilisers, cement, steel, electricity, refinery products, crude oil, and natural gas** are critical in meeting the demand for inputs across industries. The growth in these industries has held steady, reflecting a broad momentum in industrial activity.

Robust Growth in Bank Credit to Industry

- Growth in **bank credit** has kept pace with industrial growth, with a sequential surge evident since January 2022.
- While a large share of bank credit continues to be assigned to large industries, credit to **MSMEs** has also seen a significant increase in part assisted by the introduction of the **ECLGS**, which supports around 1.2 crore businesses of which 95 per cent are MSMEs.
- Robust growth in credit demand combined with rising capacity utilisation and investment in manufacturing underscores businesses' optimism regarding future demand.

All segments within the manufacturing sector except the textile industry witnessed growth in credit offtake in November 2022. While segments such as "Petroleum, coal products and nuclear fuels", "Rubber, plastic and their products", and "Engineering" have had a steady credit appetite, the improvement in growth of credit to the cement and construction sectors over the past year reflects the improved outlook of the construction sector.

Resilient FDI inflow in Manufacturing Sector

- Annual FDI equity inflows in the manufacturing sector have been steadily increasing over the last few years. It jumped from US$ 12.1 billion in FY21 to US$ 21.3 billion in FY22 as the pandemic-driven expansionary policies of advanced economies led to a surge in global liquidity.
- The government has implemented an investor-friendly FDI policy under which FDI up to 100 per cent is permitted through automatic route in most sectors.

Industry Groups and their Challenges

Micro, Small and Medium Enterprises (MSMEs) post smart recovery from pandemic

- Through the **Aatma Nirbhar Bharat Package**, the government has taken multiple steps to cushion the economic impact of the pandemic on MSMEs.

- Some of the measures undertaken include the modification of the definition of MSMEs; the provision of subordinate debt for stressed MSMEs, equity infusion through **Self Reliant India fund**; the waiving of the global tender requirement for procurement; launching of the **Udyam portal** for MSME registration, a paperless, zero-cost registration portal that is based on self-declaration and only requires Aadhaar.
- The government's initiative of the **Samadhaan Portal,** set up under the **Micro, Small and Medium Enterprises Development (MSMED) Act** to monitor the outstanding dues to the MSME sector, is helping MSMEs in resolving their cashflow difficulties.
- The government has also initiated the **'Raising and Accelerating MSME Performance' scheme (RAMP)** in FY23.

Electronics industry to be a key driver of manufacturing output and export

- Initiatives and incentives provided by the government to nurture and enhance the electronics manufacturing base include the **PLI scheme for Large Scale Electronics Manufacturing, the PLI scheme for IT hardware, the Scheme for Promotion of Manufacturing of Electronic Components and Semiconductors (SPECS).**
- Under the **Programme for Development of Semiconductors and Display Manufacturing Ecosystem** in India, the Cabinet approved the comprehensive development of a sustainable semiconductor and display ecosystem in the country.

Coal Industry: Key in maintaining energy self-reliance during uncertain times

- Different measures have been initiated towards achieving self-reliance in coal production, including private participation in coal production, FDI under the automatic route, auctioning of coal blocks for commercial production, expansion of existing mines and opening of new mines, greater use of mass production technology in mining, mechanisation of loading, development of evacuation infrastructure etc.

- The enhanced domestic coal production is expected to meet domestic coal demand, replace substitutable imports, and escalate exports.

Re-invigorated infrastructure sector & construction activity to drive steel industry

- The country is now a global force in steel production and the 2nd largest crude steel producer in the world.
- Domestic steel makers' stable credit profiles, deleveraged balance sheets, and robust cash accrual support continue to support their capex.
- Iron and steel exports moderated in the first eight months of the current fiscal owing to a slowdown in the global economy, particularly in Europe and China, and export duty levied to enhance domestic availability. Yet, iron and steel exports are higher by 20 per cent over the corresponding pre-pandemic levels of FY20.

Government support to help textile Industry weather current challenges

- The Textile industry is one of the country's most significant sources of employment generation, with an estimated 4.5 crore people directly engaged in this sector, including a large number of women and the rural population.
- To develop integrated large-scale and modern industrial infrastructure facilities for the entire value chain of the textile industry, the government approved the setting up of seven **PM Mega Integrated Textile Region and Apparel (PM MITRA) Parks.** The parks will not only reduce logistics costs and improve the competitiveness of Indian Textiles but also boost employment generation, attract domestic investment and FDI, and position India firmly in the global textile market. The parks are expected to create a total of one lakh direct and two lakh indirect employment.
- Further, to boost the production capacity, the government launched the **Textile PLI Scheme**.

Growth momentum in pharmaceuticals industry sustains after the pandemic

- India is ranked **3rd worldwide** in the production of pharma products by volume and 14th by value. The nation is the largest provider of generic medicines globally, occupying a 20 per cent share in global supply by volume, and is the leading vaccine manufacturer globally with a market share of 60 per cent.
- The government has undertaken various measures to improve the infrastructural facilities of the pharma sector. The concerned scheme, Strengthening the Pharmaceutical Industry (SPI), was launched in 2022.

India becomes the world's 3rd largest automobile market

- The automobile sector is a key driver of India's economic growth. In December 2022, India became the 3rd largest automobile market, surpassing Japan and Germany in terms of sales.
- The sector's importance is gauged by the fact that it contributes 7.1 per cent to the overall GDP and 49 per cent to the manufacturing GDP while generating direct and indirect employment of 3.7 crore at the end of 2021.

India's Prospects as a Key Player in the Global Value Chain

- The three primary assets to capitalise on this unique opportunity are
  - the potential for significant domestic demand
  - the Government's drive to encourage manufacturing
  - a distinct demographic edge, including a considerable proportion of the young workforce
- The 'Make-in-India' Initiative was launched in 2014 to make India a hub for manufacturing, design, and innovation. Since then, it has facilitated investment, fostered innovation and built world-class infrastructure.

Make in India 2.0 and the PLI schemes

- To further enhance India's integration in the global value chain, **'Make in India 2.0'** is now focusing on 27 sectors, which include 15 manufacturing sectors and 12 service sectors.
- In pursuit of the objectives of the **Make-in-India programme** and with a vision to achieve **Aatmanirbharta,** the government launched the PLI scheme. The scheme is expected to attract a capex of approximately ₹3 lakh crore over the next five years.
- PLI Scheme across these key specific sectors is poised to make Indian manufacturers globally competitive, attract investment in the areas of core competency and cutting-edge technology; ensure efficiencies; create economies of scale; and make India an integral part of the global value chain. The scheme will benefit the MSME ecosystem in the country.

Flipping and Reverse Flipping: the recent developments in Start-ups

- India ranks amongst the largest start-up ecosystems in the world.
- Various targeted initiatives of the Government have given a major boost to start-ups. For instance,
- Under the **Start-up India Initiative**, eligible companies get recognised as Start-ups by DPIIT to access a host of tax benefits, easier compliance, and IPR (Intellectual Property Rights) fast-tracking.
- As part of the umbrella schemes of the **National Initiative for Developing and Harnessing Innovations**
- **(NIDHI)** and **Atal Innovation Mission (AIM)**, entrepreneurship and innovation are fostered across the start-up ecosystem in the country.
- The Fund of Funds for Start-ups (FFS) and Credit Guarantee Scheme for Start-ups (CGSS) support seed funding and successive credit needs.

India and Industry 4.0

- The advent of the fourth industrial revolution or industry 4.0 as it's commonly referred to, has begun.

- The transformation integrates new technologies such as cloud computing, IoT, machine learning, and artificial intelligence (AI) into manufacturing processes, leading to efficiencies across the value chain.
- While the adoption of these technologies in the Indian manufacturing sector is underway, large-scale adoption is yet to happen. However, an enabling environment is rapidly developing.
- In recent years, India has made significant strides in internet penetration which is one of the key requisites of industry 4.0.
- The push towards self-reliance in semiconductor technology and production will help India erect another pillar of this revolution-hyper-efficient processing technology.
- The government is cognisant of the importance of industry 4.0 in achieving the goals of Aatmanirbharta and its ambitions of becoming a key player in global value chains.
- A few initiatives by the government include the **SAMARTH** (Smart Advanced Manufacturing and Rapid Transformation Hubs) **Udyog Bharat 4.0** under the **Ministry of Heavy Industries and Public Enterprises,** which aims to encourage technological solutions to Indian manufacturing units through awareness programmes and demonstrations.
- Another initiative is the establishment of the Centre for Fourth Industrial Revolution in India in 2018, which looks to develop policy frameworks for emerging technologies.

10. SERVICES: SOURCE OF STRENGTH

Trends in High-Frequency Indicators

- India's services sector, which was in contraction due to first by Covid-19, later Russia-Ukraine conflict witnessed an uptick and expanded in December 2022.
- **Bank Credit:** Bank credit witnessed significant growth since October 2021 due to vaccination coverage and services sector recovery.

NBFCs shifted to bank borrowings because of high bond yields and hence, its credit grew.

- **Services Trade:**
  - World services trade volume remain strong by spending on travel, Information and Communication Technology (ICT) services, and financial services.
  - However, Financial and ICT Services have been so far most resilient to the slowing global economy, whereas, construction services and container shipping fell into contraction territory.
  - Software exports have remained relatively resilient during the Covid-19 pandemic as well as amid current geopolitical uncertainties, driven by higher demand for digital support, cloud services, and infrastructure modernisation catering to new challenges.
- **Foreign Direct Investment (FDI) in Services**
  - To facilitate investment, various measures have been undertaken by the Government, such as the launch of the **National Single-Window system**, a one-stop solution for approvals and clearances needed by investors, entrepreneurs, and businesses. India will be included in JP Morgan's Government Bond Index-Emerging Markets (GBI-EM) on June 28, 2024.
  - To ensure the liberalisation of investment in various industries, the Government has permitted 100 per cent foreign participation in telecommunication services, including all services and infrastructure providers, through the Automatic Route.

Major Services: Sub-Sector-Wise Performance

- **Travel and tourism** are two of the largest industries in India, with a total contribution of about US$ 178 billion to the country's GDP.
  - **Medical Tourism sector** is predicted to increase at a CAGR of 21.1% from 2020-27.
  - **Travel market** in India is projected to reach US$ 125 billion by FY27 from an estimated US$ 75 billion in FY20.
  - **International tourist** arrivals are expected to reach 30.5 million by 2028.

Making India an attractive tourist destination

- National Integrated Database of Hospitality Industry (NIDHI): This database will help in creating policies and strategies for the promotion and development of tourism at various destinations.
- SAATHI was launched in association with the Quality Council of India to restrict any further transmission of the virus while providing accommodation and other services post-lockdown.
- For better connectivity, **Regional Connectivity Scheme (RCS-UDAN)** was launched.

- **Real Estate:** In the Union Budget 2023-24, a commitment of ₹ 79,000 crore (US$ 9.64 billion) for PM Awas Yojana has been announced, which represents a 66% increase compared to the last year.
- **E-Commerce**: India's e-commerce market is projected to grow at 18% annually till 2025. The growth of e-commerce in India is being driven by the expansion into new segments, like grocery and general merchandise, which has attracted a wider customer base.
- **Digital financial services**: The use of innovative technologies and digital solutions is boosting financial inclusion and personalizing financial products.
  - The foundation of digital financial services in India has been established with the **JAM trinity, UPI and other regulations, and the pandemic has driven even greater adoption of these services to be utilized by banks, NBFCs, insurers as well as fintech.**

Account Aggregator Framework

- The Account Aggregator (AA) is an NBFC that collects the financial information of customers and transfers them from one financial institution to another, after the explicit consent of the customers. Entities can enroll as either a Financial Information Provider (FIP) or Financial Information User (FIU) regulated by a financial sector regulator.
- The RBI has issued regulations for AA in the form of a Master Direction and has currently granted registration to 6 companies as AA.

11. EXTERNAL SECTOR: WATCHFUL AND HOPEFUL

Introduction

- India's external sector has been buffeted by shocks and uncertainty manifested in terms of elevated, though now easing global commodity prices; tightening international financial conditions; heightening financial market volatility; reversal of capital flows; currency depreciation, and looming global growth and trade slowdown.
- During FY23 India's exports have displayed resilience on the back of record levels of exports in FY22.
  - Petroleum products, gems & jewellery, organic & inorganic chemicals, drugs & pharmaceuticals were among the leading export items.
- However, the slowdown in Indian exports is inevitable in a slowing global economy characterised by
  - slowing global trade
  - pressure encountered by Balance of Payments (BoP)
  - widened Current Account Deficit (CAD)
- Though the fortified shock absorbers of India's external sector are in place to cushion the global headwinds be it the
  - formidable forex reserves
  - sustainable external debt indicators
  - market-determined exchange rate

However, after all the shocks, it has been able to face these headwinds from a position of strength on the back of strong macroeconomic fundamentals and buffers.

- **India's growing and diversifying trade:** International trade has been an important pillar of the resilience of India's external sector. Trade as a percentage of GDP for India was in the range of 12-15 per cent in the 1980s; 16-25 per cent in the 1990s and 25-50 per cent in the 2000s.

- **Trends in Merchandise Trade:** India achieved an all-time high annual merchandise export of US$ 422.0 billion in FY22.
- **Trade in Services:** India maintained its dominance in the world services trade in FY22. While strong revenues in major information technology (IT) companies from various segments such as retail and consumer business; communications and media; healthcare; and banking, financial and insurance services drove the growth in software exports, a significant pick-up in engineering, and research and development related services boosted the growth in business services exports during the quarter.
- **Foreign Trade Policy:** India's Foreign Trade Policy (FTP) has, conventionally, been formulated for five years at a time. The focus of the FTP has been to provide a framework of rules and procedures for exports and imports and a set of incentives for promoting exports.

Initiatives to enhance trade

- **Focus on Agricultural Products:** India's agricultural exports achieved the highest ever export in FY22 reaching US$ 37.8 billion and it continued to perform well in FY23 with exports of US$ 26.8 billion during April-November 2022 backed by an effective agriculture export policy.
- **Interest Equalisation Scheme:** This Scheme was formulated to give benefit in the interest rates being charged by the banks to the exporters on their pre- and post-shipment rupee export credits.
- **Remission of Duties and Taxes on Exported Products (RoDTEP) Scheme:** The scheme seeks remission of Central, State and Local duties/taxes/levies at different stages at the Central, State, and local level, which are incurred in the process of manufacturing and distribution of exported products, but are currently not being refunded under any other duty remission scheme.
- **Export Credit Guarantee:** The Export Credit Guarantee Corporation (ECGC) supports Indian exporters and banks by providing export credit insurance services.

- **Krishi Udan Scheme:** Krishi Udan Scheme was launched in August 2020 on international and national routes to assist farmers in transporting agricultural products so that it improves their value realisation along with kisan rail this greatly facilated in improving market access of farm produce.
- **Trade Infrastructure for Export Scheme:** The Government has been implementing the Trade Infrastructure for Export Scheme since FY18 to assist Central and State Government Agencies in the creation of appropriate infrastructure for the growth of exports from the States.
- **Districts as Export Hubs – One District One Product Initiative:** The Districts as Export Hubs-ODOP initiative is aimed at targeting export promotion, manufacturing, and employment generation at the grassroots level, making the states and districts meaningful stakeholders and active participants in making India an export powerhouse thereby contributing to the Aatm Nirbhar mission and achieving the vision of Make in India for the world and being Vocal for Local.

Free Trade Agreements

- FTAs or RTAs in terms of the WTO rules are economic instruments available to a country for leveraging its competencies in trade and investment. As of June 2016, all WTO members now have at least one RTA in force. There has been a substantial rise in the number of trade agreements with 355 notifications of RTAs having been made to the WTO (As of 1 December 2022).
- Many WTO members continue to be involved in negotiations to create new RTAs, which are mostly bilateral. However, a recent development has been negotiations and new agreements among more than two WTO members.
- The limited progress in the multilateral trade negotiations at the WTO is one of the reasons responsible for the increase in FTAs. FTAs are viewed favourably by trading countries in comparison to multilateral negotiation at the WTO forum as they are easy to negotiate and provide flexibility to factor in geopolitical considerations.

- The purpose of RTAs is to lower tariffs on goods and services and increase cooperation between trading partners with the aim of increasing trade, lower prices for consumers, and provide enhanced export opportunities for producers. RTAs can also have a larger impact on the economy.
- FTAs are positively correlated with direct domestic value-added exports, as well as forward and backward participation in global value chains.

Conclusion

To sum up, while India's external sector faces challenges, it is performing relatively better as compared to many of its peers as it has inbuilt shock absorbers to weather them.

12. PHYSICAL & DIGITAL INFRASTRUCTURE - LIFTING POTENTIAL GROWTH

Introduction

As India completes 75 years of Independence, the nation is evolving into a prominent force in the global economic order. India is the world's fifth largest economy and the prospect of steady progress in the coming years is bright.

Government Interventions

In order to increase the private sector participation in creation of new infrastructure and development of existing ones, the government took initiatives like **Public-Private Partnership (PPP)**, **National Infrastructure Pipeline (NIP)** and **National Monetisation Pipeline (NMP)**. In addition to this, as part of the structural reforms with the objective to enhance efficiencies and cost competitiveness, **Gati Shakti and National Logistics Policy (NLP)** were also launched.

- **Public-Private Partnerships (PPPs):** In India, private participation in infrastructure programmes supports several PPP models, including management contracts like Build-Operate-Transfer (BOT), Design, Built, Finance, Operate and Transfer (DBFOT), Rehabilitate, Operate and Transfer (ROT), Hybrid Annuity Model (HAM), and Toll, Operate and Transfer (TOT) model.
- **National Infrastructure Pipeline (NIP):** The government launched the National Infrastructure Pipeline (NIP) with a forward-looking approach and with a projected infrastructure investment of around ₹111 lakh crore during FY20-25 to provide high quality infrastructure across the country.
- **National Monetisation Pipeline:** The National Monetisation Pipeline (NMP) provides an opportunity for deleveraging balance sheets and providing fiscal space for investment in new infrastructure assets.
- **National Logistics Policy:** India aims to increase its exports manifold, logistics costs in India have been in the range of 14-18 per cent of GDP against the global benchmark of 8 per cent.

Government efforts to improve logistics ecosystem in India:

- Ude Desh ka Aam Nagrik (UDAN)
- Bharatmala
- Sagarmala
- Parvatamala
- National Rail Plan
- e-Sanchit
- Single Window Interface for Trade (SWIFT)
- Indian Customs Electronic Data Interchange Gateway (ICEGATE)
- Turant Customs

- **PM Gati Shakti:** The Plan entails creation of a common umbrella platform with all infrastructure projects pertaining to various ministries/departments incorporated within a comprehensive database for efficient planning and implementation on a real-time basis.

Developments in Physical Infrastructure Sectors

- There has been an increase in the construction of National Highways (NHs)/roads over time, with 10,457 km of roads constructed in FY22 as compared to 6,061 km in FY16.

- In FY23 (until October 2022), 4,060 km of NHs/roads were constructed, which was around 91 per cent of the achievement in the corresponding period of the previous financial year.
- Total budgetary support for investment in the sector has been increasing rapidly in the last four years and stood at around ₹1.4 lakh crore during FY23 (as of 31 October 2022).
- **ROAD:** National Highways/Road construction has increased since 2015-16, hitting unprecedented levels in 2020-21.
- **RAILWAYS:** The Indian Railways (IR), with over 68,031 route kms, is the fourth largest network in the world under single management.
- Major initiatives of the Indian Railways:
  - Mumbai-Ahmedabad High Speed Rail (MAHSR) Project
  - Dedicated Freight Corridor (DFC) Project
  - Gati Shakti Multi-Modal Cargo Terminal (GCT)
  - Induction of semi-high-speed Vande Bharat Trainsets
  - Electrical/Electronic Interlocking System
  - Development of Hyperloop technology
  - Kisan Rail
- **INLAND WATER TRANSPORT:** Inland water transport holds total navigable length of waterways in India is around 14,850 kilometres.
- **ELECTRICTITY:** In order to reduce the carbon footprint of the farm sector, Pradhan Mantri Kisan Urja Suraksha evam Utthaan Mahabhiyan (PM-KUSUM) aims to provide energy and water security, de-dieselisation the farm sector and generate additional income for farmers by producing solar power.

Developments in Digital Infrastructure

- **Telecommunications:** Today, the total telephone subscriber base in India stands at 117 crore (as of November 2022). While more than 97 per cent of the total subscribers are connected wirelessly (114.3 crore at the end of November 2022), 83.7 crore have internet connections as of June 2022. The overall tele-density in India stood at 84.8 per cent, with wide differences across states.

- **Digital Public Infrastructure:** The emergence of Digital Public Infrastructure (DPI), aimed at improving financial literacy, innovation, entrepreneurship, employment generation, and empowering beneficiaries has played a critical role in uplifting the economy and bringing it to the stature where it stands today.
- **UMANG:** Unified Mobile Application for New-Age Governance (UMANG), which enables citizens to access e-Government services offered by the Central and State Government in various sectors such as **agriculture, education, health, housing, employees, pensioners, and students' welfare, the Public Distribution System, and others**.
- **Open Network for Digital Commerce (ONDC):** ONDC aims to go beyond the current platform-centric digital commerce model where the buyer and seller can use the same platform or application for transactions.

Conclusion

The synergy between physical and digital infrastructure will be one of the defining features of India's future growth story.

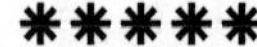

PRELIMS MCQs

Q1: Regarding India's public debt consider the following:

1. Majority of the debt is owed by the Central Government as compared to State governments.
2. Majority of the debt is characterized as being external in nature
3. Majority of the debt is of long-term nature.
4. Majority of the debt is dependent on a floating rate of interest

Select the correct answer from the code given below:

(a) 1 and 3 only

(b) 2 and 4 only

(c) 2, 3 and 4 only

(d) 1, 2, 3 and 4

Q2: Which of the following are the steps taken for an economic recovery?

1. Open market Operations
2. Managing liquidity flow in market
3. Increasing Interest rates
4. Structural reforms

Select the correct answer from the code given below:

(a) 1 and 3 only (b) 2 and 4 only

(c) 1, 2 and 3 only (d) 1, 2 and 4 only

Q3: Regarding 'supply shock', which of the following statements is/are correct?

1. Supply shocks are always negative

2. Negative supply shock causes a product's price to spike upward
3. It is caused by unforeseen events such as natural disasters or geopolitical events.

Select the correct answer using the code given below:

(a) 1 only (b) 2 and 3 only

(c) 1 and 3 only (d) 1, 2 and 3

Q4: With reference to the India's public debt, consider the following statements:

1. Indian Government is the largest holder and financier of public debt.
2. India's debt policy does not allow in the significant capital outflows from India.
3. India's public debt to GDP ratio is below 100%.
4. India's domestic ownership of public debt has played a crucial role in helping it navigate negative spillovers from international financial crises and Covid-19.

How many of the statements given above is/are correct?

(a) Only 1 (b) Only 2

(c) Only 3 (d) All 4

Q5: With reference to budget of Union Government of India, the money spent on which of the following are included in the capital expenditure?

1. Acquiring fixed and intangible assets
2. Upgrading an existing asset
3. Repairing an existing asset
4. Repayment of loan

Select the correct answer using the code given below:

(a) 1, 3 and 4 only (b) 2 and 4 only

(c) 1 and 3 only (d) 1, 2, 3 and 4

Q6: Consider the following statements:

1. The Gender Inequality Index considers three dimensions: reproductive health, empowerment, and per capita income to measure gender disparities.
2. A low GII value signifies reduced inequality between genders, and conversely, a higher value indicates greater disparity.
3. The index is computed separately for men and women, then harmonically combined to produce an aggregate measure of gender inequality.

Which of the above statements is/are correct?

(a) 1 only (b) 2 and 3 only

(c) 1 and 3 only (d) 1, 2 and 3

Q7: In which of the following circumstances, the calculation of GDP would be accurate?

1. Including net exports in the Expenditure method of GDP estimation.
2. Accounting for depreciation in the income method.
3. Including both intermediate and final good in the Value Addition method of GDP estimation.
4. Subtracting Product subsides in the GDP estimation.

Select the correct answer from the code given below:

(a) 1 and 2 only (b) 1, 2 and 3 only

(c) 2 and 4 only (d) 1, 2 and 4 only

Q8: Consider the following statements:

1. GDP takes into account of positive externalities but overlooks negative externalities.
2. It underestimates the economic activities that occur in the gig economy.
3. GDP overstates the importance of consumption relative to production in the economy.
4. It does not take into account profits earned in a nation by overseas companies

How many of the given statements indicate the failure of the GDP as the measurement of growth?

(a) Only 1 (b) Only 2
(c) Only 3 (d) All 4

Q9: Which of the following given structural reforms helped in the formalization of economy and expanding 'tax net':

1. Introduction of GST
2. Faceless Assessment and Appeal system in GST
3. Digitization of economic transactions through digital payment systems
4. Enrolment of informal sector workers on government portals.

Select the correct answer using the code given below:

(a) 2 and 3 only (b) 1, 3 and 4 only
(c) 1, 2 and 4 only (d) All of the above

Q10: Consider the following statements regarding Capital Expenditure by government in India:

1. It develops infrastructure-intensive sectors like roadways and railways.
2. It develops housing and urban affairs.
3. It strengthens aggregate demand in economy
4. It enhances crowds-in private spending in the economy

Which of the above statements is/are correct?

(a) 1, 2 and 3 only (b) 1, 3 and 4 only
(c) 1, 2 and 4 only (d) All of the above

Q11: Which of the following given structural reforms helped in the formalization of economy and expanding 'tax net':

1. Introduction of GST
2. Faceless Assessment and Appeal system in GST
3. Digitization of economic transactions through digital payment systems
4. Enrolment of informal sector workers on government portals.

Select the correct answer using the code given below:

(a) 2 and 3 only (b) 1, 3 and 4 only

(c) 1, 2 and 4 only (d) All of the above

Q12: Consider the following statements regarding Capital Expenditure by government in India:

1. It develops infrastructure-intensive sectors like roadways and railways.
2. It develops housing and urban affairs.
3. It strengthens aggregate demand in economy
4. It enhances crowds-in private spending in the economy

Which of the above statements is/are correct?

(a) 1, 2 and 3 only (b) 1, 3 and 4 only

(c) 1, 2 and 4 only (d) All of the above

Q13: Consider the following statements regarding the Government Security (G-Sec):

1. A Government Security is a tradeable instrument which cannot have the maturity of more than one year.
2. In India, only the Central Government issues both treasury bills and dated securities.
3. Cash Management Bills are a type of G-Sec but with lower maturity period than that of the Treasury bills.
4. Treasury bills are zero coupon securities and pay no interest.

How many of the above statements is/are correct?

(a) None (b) Only 1

(c) Only 2 (d) Only 2

Q14: With reference to the term Discretionary fiscal stimulus, consider the following statements:

1. It signifies a rise in the fiscal deficit due to a slowdown in economic growth.
2. It functions as an automatic stabilizer in economic downturns, adjusting fiscal policies to mitigate economic fluctuations.

Which of the statements given above is/are correct?

(a) Only 1 (b) Only 2

(c) Both 1 and 2 (d) Neither 1 nor 2

Explanation:

- **Statement 1 is incorrect:** Discretionary fiscal stimulus' refers to an increase in the fiscal deficit caused by government policy as distinct from an increase caused by slowing growth. The government's focus thus so far has been on reassuring the financial markets that the fiscal will not spin out of control. It has kept the 'discretionary fiscal stimuli down to 1% of GDP', a figure that is most modest about that of many other economies especially developed economies.
- **Statement 2 is incorrect:** Discretionary fiscal policies are different from automatic fiscal stabilizers. Automatic stabilizers occur wherein in a recession a government automatically spends more because there are more claiming unemployment benefits. However, the government may feel these automatic stabilizers are insufficient and so they decide to increase public work spending schemes too.

Q15: Consider the following statements regarding fiscal policy:

1. States need not to take prior approval from the Centre for their further borrowings even if they have taken debt from the Centre.
2. Off-budget borrowings constitute one of the largest items in the fiscal deficit of the Government as interest payment for such borrowings is made out of the consolidated fund.

Which of the above statements is/are correct?

(a) 1 only (b) 2 only

(c) Both 1 and 2 (d) Neither 1 nor 2

ANSWERS									
1. (b)	**2. (d)**	**3. (b)**	**4. (d)**	**5. (d)**	**6. (b)**	**7. (d)**	**8. (c)**	**9. (b)**	**10. (d)**
11. (b)	**12. (d)**	**13. (d)**	**14. (d)**	**15. (d)**					

*****

MAINS PRACTICE QUESTIONS

Q1: What do you understand by money multiplier? What are the determinants of money multiplier?

Q2: Rural-Urban Inflation Differential is a key component in the overall inflation for the economy. Elaborate?

Q3: Besides the push to physical infrastructure, emphasis on public digital infrastructure is the key to enhance the economic potential of individuals and businesses. Discuss?

Q4: Identify the growth magnets that will propel India's growth in the ongoing decade and give reasons for their contribution.

Q5: Highlight the sustainable practices in agriculture and allied sectors and their role in meeting the increasing demand for fish products. Discuss environmental considerations, technological innovations, and government support in this sector.

Q6: Analyze the role of the services sector, such as IT and tourism, in shaping the invisibles component of a country's balance of payments.

Q7: Analyse how can a country manage a sustained current account deficit without compromising economic stability?

Q8: Analyze the contribution of the private sector in promoting formal employment.

Q9: Discuss the effectiveness of rural employment generation programs. Evaluate schemes aimed at creating jobs in rural areas and their impact on reducing urban-rural migration for employment?

Q10: Evaluate policies aimed at transitioning to a green economy and their impact on job creation in environmentally friendly sectors.

*****

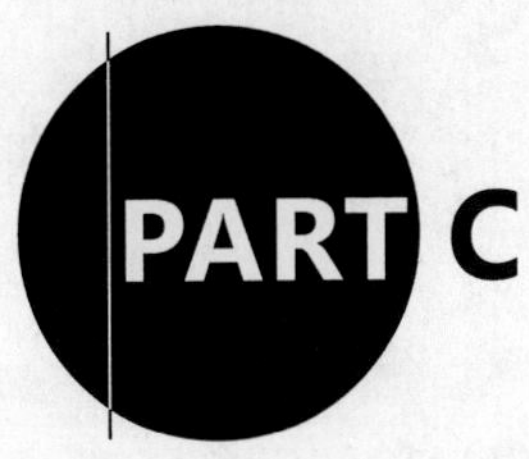

INTERIM BUDGET 2024

KEY-TERMS

- **Direct Taxes:**

  These are taxes paid directly to the party that levied them. For example - Income Tax.

- **Indirect Tax:**

  It is the tax levied on the consumption of goods and services. It is not directly levied on the income of a person. For example - Service Tax, Excise Duty, Value Added Tax (VAT), Custom Duty, Stamp Duty, etc.

- **Primary Agricultural Credit Society:**

  It is a basic unit and smallest co-operative credit institutions in India. It is a village-level institution that works directly with rural residents. It encourages agriculturists to save, accepts deposits from them, makes loans to deserving borrowers, and collects repayments.

- **Blue Sheet:**

  The Blue Sheet in the Union Budget is a confidential blueprint containing crucial numbers, updated throughout the Budget preparation, and safeguarded by the joint secretary of the Finance Minister.

- **Effective Capital Expenditure:**

  Effective Capital Expenditure (Eff-Capex) refers to the sum of Capital Expenditure and Grants-in-Aid for Creation of Capital Assets.

- **Capital Budget:**

  The Capital Budget deals with capital receipts (like disinvestment, loans) and capital expenditures (such as developing health facilities, roads, acquiring land). It reflects the government's investment and financing activities for long-term projects and assets.

- **Revenue Budget:**

The Revenue Budget encompasses revenue receipts (tax-related income, dividends/interest on investments, service fees) and revenue expenditures. It covers ongoing government operations, debt interest, and subsidies. It reflects the day-to-day functioning and financial transactions of the government.

- **Consolidated Fund of India:**

It includes revenues received and expenses incurred by the government in a financial year, excluding exceptional expenses like disaster management. Government cannot access it without Parliament approval.

- **Rebate:**

Rebate is a reduction in the total income tax you owe, encouraging economic activity by lightening the tax load for individuals.

- **TDS (Tax Deducted at Source):**

TDS is like a silent way the government collects tax. For example, when banks transfer interest income to account, they deduct a certain percentage as tax before giving you the money. It ensures that taxes are collected in a timely manner.

- **TCS (Tax Collection at Source):**

TCS is like a little extra amount collected as tax by a seller from the buyer at the time of sale. This amount is then deposited with the tax authority. It ensures that taxes are collected right when a transaction happens.

- **Annual Financial Statement:**

Under Article 112 of the Constitution of India, the central government is mandated to present to Parliament an Annual Financial Statement. This statement outlines the estimated receipts and expenditures for every financial year. Typically, this document is categorized into three main funds: Consolidated Fund, Contingency Fund, and Public Account.

■ Money Bill:

A Money Bill is a specific category of Finance Bill that addresses matters related to taxes, revenues, and government expenditure. For a bill to be treated as a Money Bill, it must contain specified matters under Article 110(1)(a) to (g) of the Constitution of India. Importantly, a Money Bill can only be presented in the Lok Sabha.

■ Finance Bill:

A Finance Bill is a critical component of the Budget documentation, encompassing all details related to government revenue, expenditures, and allocations for a specific financial year. It provides insights into new taxes, as well as modifications to existing tax structures. Presented for a one-year period, once the Bill is passed, it transforms into the Finance Act. The preparation of the Finance Bill is in accordance with the provisions under Article 117 of the Constitution of India.

■ Budget Estimates:

Budget Estimates refer to the projected funds allocated to various ministries, departments, sectors, and schemes of the central government in the Union Budget. These estimates determine the expected costs over a specified time period and outline how and where the allocated money will be utilized.

■ Revised Estimates:

In comparison to Budget estimates, some ministries or departments may require more funds than initially anticipated as the financial year progresses. This necessitates modifications to the allocations announced in the Union Budget, termed as Revised Estimates. The government reviews and adjusts these allocations as needed based on evolving financial needs.

CHAPTER SUMMARY

India's Finance Ministry presented the country's **Interim Budget** for 2024 at a time when the overall economic landscape appears stable, backed by strong macroeconomic data. The budget outlines a multi-pronged economic management strategy, including infrastructure development, digital public infrastructure, and tax reforms. Given that 2024 is an election year, the **Vote on Account or Interim Budget** would merely be an interim approval to spend money, without any major tax or policy changes expected. Noting that India's economy will see an "unprecedented" development, four major areas of focus for the government have been highlighted:

- Poverty
- Youth
- Women
- Farmers

Important Estimation (key numbers):

- **Fiscal Consolidation:** FY24 fiscal deficit is estimated at 5.8% of GDP, below the budged 5.9%. The government pegged the FY25 target at 5.1%, with an aim to reduce it to 4.5% by FY26.
- **Capital expenditure**: It will rise by 11.1% to 11.11 trillion rupees ($133.9 billion) in fiscal year 2025, while tax revenue for the year would be 38.31 trillion rupees ($461.7 billion).
- **Borrowings:** The administration aims to borrow ₹14.13 trillion ($170 billion) in the fiscal year starting April 1.
- **Revenue Receipts**: The revenue receipts for the current fiscal at ₹30.03 lakh crore are expected to be higher than the Budget Estimate, reflecting strong growth momentum and formalisation in the economy.

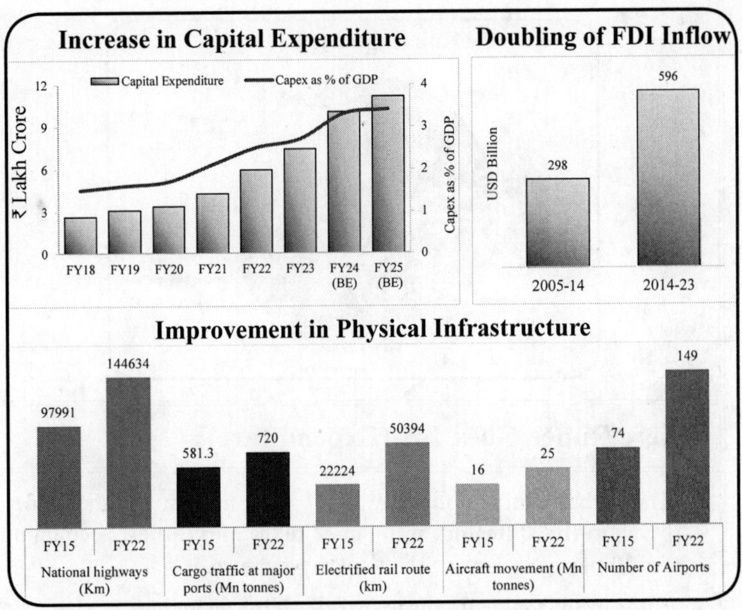

- **Infrastructure:** The outlay for infrastructure has been increased by 17% to ₹11.11 lakh crore, or 3.4% of GDP, over the revised estimate of ₹9.5 lakh crore in FY24.

Below is the breakup of where the government gets its money from and where does it spends on:

Where Rupee Come From? (Receipts)

The Budget stated that

- **Borrowings and other liabilities** constitute the highest income procured by the Centre, 28 per cent of the total income.
  - **Income Tax** (18 per cent)
  - **GST** (18 per cent)
  - **Corporation Tax** (17 per cent)
- Non-tax receipts like **rent, penalties and fines** comprised 7 per cent of the total income.
- **Union Excise Duties** (5 per cent), Customs (4 per cent) and Non-Debt Capital Receipts (1 per cent).

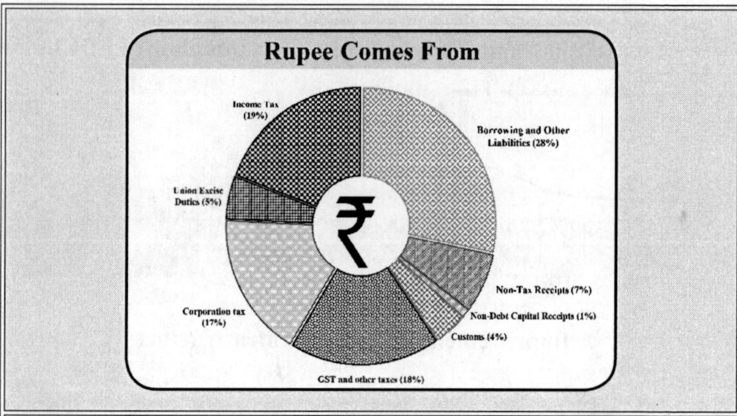

Where Rupee Goes To? (Expenditure)

- The highest amount goes towards paying interest and the money given to **the states in the form of taxes and duties**, accounting for **20 per cent each** of the total expenditure.
- **Allocation towards the central sector schemes** is the next expense comprising 16 per cent of the total expenditure.
- Other Expenditures (9 per cent).
- **Defence, Central Sponsored Schemes and Finance Commission** and other transfers (at 8 per cent each).
- **Subsidies** (6 per cent).

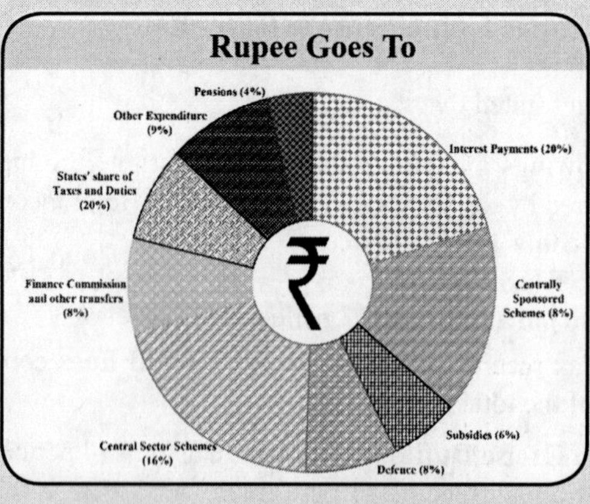

The Interim Budget 2024 unveiled a series of transformative initiatives aimed at bolstering India's growth, development, and global standing. Here's a comprehensive look at the key highlights:

KEY-TAKEAWAYS

Taxes:

- No changes in tax slabs in keeping with convention; FY25 tax receipts seen at ₹ 26.02 lakh crore.
- In a major announcement, the government has announced withdrawal of all outstanding disputed direct tax demands up to ₹ 25,000 for the period up to financial year 2009-10 and up to ₹ 10,000 for financial years 2010-11 to 2014-15.
- The only major change to taxation was tabled with respect to start-ups and investments made by **sovereign wealth or pension funds**, alongside tax exemption on certain income of some **IFSC units** – which are expiring on March 31.

Achievements of Taxation Reforms

Direct Tax Collections more than trebled in last 10 years

Number of return filers swelled to 2.4 times

Faster refunds: Reduction in average processing time of returns from 93 days (2013-14) to 10 days (2023-24)

Average monthly Gross GST collections doubled to ₹1.66 lakh crore in FY24

Increase in tax buoyancy of State revenue from 0.72 (2012-16) to 1.22 in the post-GST period (2017-23)

Benefit to consumers: Reduction in logistics cost and prices of most goods and services

Railways

The **Union Budget 2023** proposed a record budgetary allocation of ₹2.40 lakh crore for the Indian Railways.

- In a bid to improve operations of passenger trains, the government announced three major economic railway corridor programmes to improve logistics efficiency and reduce cost —
  - energy, mineral and cement corridors
  - port connectivity corridors
  - high traffic density corridors
- **Enhancing Passenger Safety and Comfort:** The government is set to convert a staggering 40,000 standard rail bogies into state-of-the-art **Vande Bharat coaches**, elevating the safety, convenience, and comfort of passengers across the nation.

Impact:

- The development of commodity-specific economic rail corridors can de-congest existing lines, mostly in the eastern part of the country.
- This is supportive of faster freight movement and turnaround times and should help reduce the logistics cost for India from 12 per cent of GDP, improving competitiveness, especially manufacturing, against peers.

State of Indian Railways:

- India is projected to account for 40% of the total global share of rail activity by 2050. In 2023-24, traffic revenue is estimated to be Rs 2,64,600 crore, comprising 99.8% of the total revenue.
- Government has allowed 100% FDI in the railway sector.
- Indian Railways is developing and creating technology in areas such as signalling and telecommunication with 15,000 kms being converted into automatic signaling and 37,000 kms to be fitted with **'KAVACH', the domestically developed Train Collision Avoidance System.**

Energy

- **Rooftop Solarisation:** Rooftop solar project to give 1 crore households 300 units of free electricity per month. **Coal gasification and liquification** of 100 million tonne to be set up by 2030. New scheme of bio manufacturing, biofoundry to be launched.

> - **Impact:** This will help save up to ₹15,000-18,000 annually for households from free solar electricity and selling the surplus to the distribution companies.

- The government will expand the **electric vehicle ecosystem** to support charging infra, and e-buses for public transport networks will be encouraged.
- The blending of compressed biogas into compressed natural gas for transport and piped natural gas will be mandatory.
- **Bio-manufacturing and biofoundry scheme** will be launched to provide environment-friendly alternatives for bio-degradable production.
- **Green Energy:** Towards meeting the commitment to 'net zero' by 2070, the following measures were announced:
  - **Viability gap funding** will be provided for harnessing offshore wind energy potential for the initial capacity of one giga-watt.
  - **Coal gasification and liquification capacity** of 100 MT will be set up by 2030. This will also help in reducing imports of **natural gas, methanol, and ammonia**.

ENERGY

India's Power Sector Transformation:

India's power sector has undergone a remarkable transformation, aimed at providing reliable, affordable, and sustainable energy to its people.

- With the addition of **over 175 GW of generation capacity** in the past 9 years, India has transitioned from a power deficit to a power surplus nation.
- **India stands 4th globally in Renewable Energy Installed Capacity**, with 43% of its total installed electricity capacity coming from non-fossil energy sources.
- **Pradhan Mantri Sahaj Bijli Har Ghar Yojana (SAUBHAGYA)** initiative has provided electricity connections to **2.86 crore unelectrified households** since September 25, 2017, both in rural and urban areas.

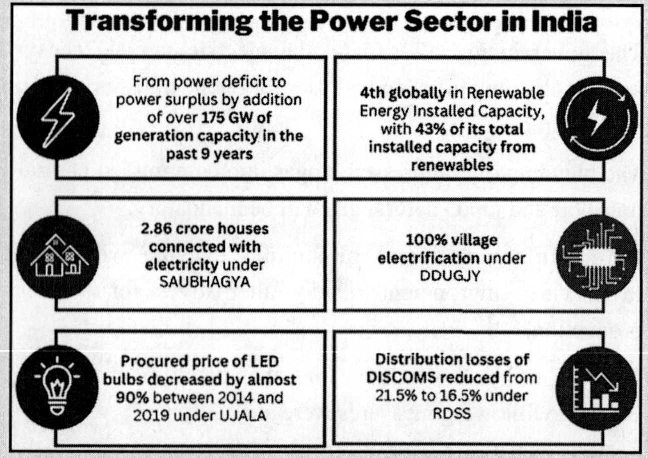

- To improve the quality and reliability of power supply in rural areas, **Deen Dayal Upadhyaya Gram Jyoti Yojana (DDUGJY)** was launched in 2014. The DDUGJY program achieved **100% village electrification** on April 28, 2018.
- Under the **Unnat Jyoti by Affordable LEDs for All (UJALA)** scheme, the procured price of LED bulbs decreased by almost 90% between 2014 and 2019, from ₹ 310 to ₹ 39.90. So far, **over 36.86 crore LED bulbs** have been distributed under this scheme.
- To enhance the efficiency of power distribution, the government has implemented initiatives like the **Restructured Distribution Sector Scheme (RDSS)**.

Agriculture and Food Processing

Welfare of Farmers-*Annadata*

Direct financial assistance to 11.8 crore farmers under PM-KISAN

Crop Insurance to 4 crore farmers under PM Fasal Bima Yojana

Integration 1,361 mandis under e-NAM, supporting trading volume of ₹ 3 lakh crore

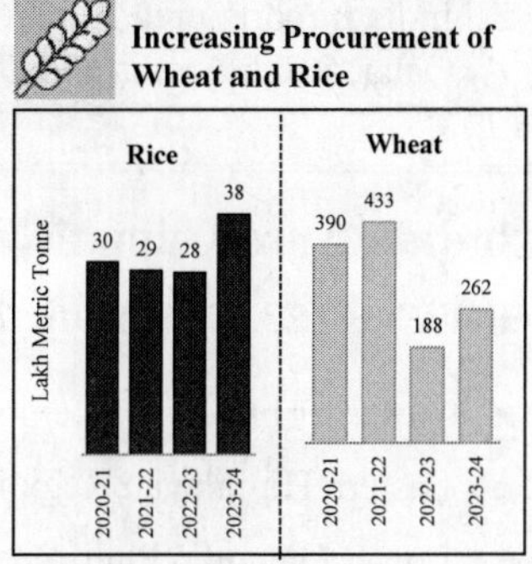

- The government announced that the efforts for value addition in the agricultural sector and boosting farmers' income will be stepped up.
- **Pradhan Mantri Kisan Sampada Yojana** has benefitted 38 lakh farmers and generated 10 lakh employment.
- **Pradhan Mantri Formalisation of Micro Food Processing Enterprises Yojana** has assisted 2.4 lakh SHGs and sixty thousand individuals with credit linkages.
- **Promotion of post-harvest activities:** Other schemes are complementing the efforts for reducing post-harvest losses and improving productivity and incomes.
- **Expansion of Nano DAP application**: Following the success of nano urea, Nano DAP application on various crops will be expanded across all **agro-climatic zones.**

DAP

- India is among the world's largest buyers of fertiliser, besides China, Brazil, and the US.
- **India imports four types of fertilisers:**
  - Urea
  - diammonium phosphate (DAP)
  - muriate of potash (MOP)

- nitrogen-phosphorous-potassium (NPK)

- India, the top importer of urea, imports about 30% of its average 35 million tonnes of annual consumption of the crop nutrient.
- India imports urea from a number of countries, including Oman, Qatar, Saudi Arabia and United Arab Emirates.

India's Agro-Climatic Zones

India has 15 Agro-climatic Zones as given below:

- Western Himalayan Region
- Eastern Himalayan Region
- Lower Gangetic Plain Region
- Middle Gangetic Plain Region
- Upper Gangetic Plains Region
- Trans-Ganga Plains Region
- Eastern Plateau and Hills
- Central Plateau and Hills
- Western Plateau and Hills
- Southern Plateau and Hills
- Eastern Coastal Plains and Hills
- Western Coastal Plains and Ghats
- Gujarat Plains and Hills
- Western Dry Region
- Island Region

- **Aatmanirbhar Oilseeds Abhiyan**: Strategy formulation to achieve self-reliance in oilseeds through research, adoption of modern farming techniques, market linkages, and crop insurance.
- **Matsya Sampada**: Promotion of investments in fisheries to generate employment opportunities, with a separate department set up for fisheries under the government's initiative.

Pradhan Mantri Matsya Sampada Yojana (PMMSY)

Introduced by the Department of Fisheries, Pradhan Mantri Matsya Sampada Yojana (PMMSY), the aim of the scheme is to bring about Blue Revolution through the sustainable development of the fisheries sector over a period of five years (2020-2025).

Defence

- **Defence Outlay:** A substantial 11.1% increase in the Defence outlay, amounting to ₹ 11,11,111 crore, demonstrates the government's dedication to national security.
  - **Strengthening Deep Tech in Defence**: The government is set to launch a comprehensive plan to strengthen deep tech capabilities in the Defence sector, ensuring India's security and technological prowess.

The Central government aims to take India's defence exports up to US$ 5 Bn by 2024-25.

Defence Sector of India

- The Indian Defence sector is the second largest armed force in the world.
- The Government has identified the Defence and Aerospace sector as a focus area for the 'Aatmanirbhar Bharat' or Self-Reliant India initiative.
- **Recent Initiatives**
  - To promote export and liberalise foreign investments FDI in Defence Sector has been enhanced up to 74% through the Automatic Route and 100% by Government Route.
  - The government has also announced 2 dedicated Defence Industrial Corridors in the States of Tamil Nadu and Uttar Pradesh to act as clusters of defence manufacturing that leverage existing infrastructure, and human capital.

- To enable innovation within Defence & Aerospace eco-system there are supportive government schemes such as **iDEX (Innovations for Defence Excellence) and DTIS (Defence Testing Infrastructure Scheme).**

Housing

- The government plans to launch a scheme for **deserving sections of middle class** living in **rented houses or slums** to build their own houses. Details are awaited.
- The government also aims to make 2 crore houses in the next five years under the **PM Awas Yojana-Grameen** and is close to achieving the 3 crore target.
- **Housing for the middle class** - The Government will launch a scheme to help deserving sections of the middle class, living in rented houses or slums, or chawls and unauthorized colonies, to buy or build their own houses. This is likely to free encroachment areas like slums for easier redevelopment.
- The Finance Minister also announced 2 crore more houses under the **Pradhan Mantri Awas Yojana – Gramin (PMAY-G).**

Pradhan Mantri Gramin Awaas Yojana is a flagship programme of the Central Government in its mission to provide affordable housing for all.

Women

- **Empowering Women (Triple Talaq Ban and Legislative Representation):** The government's commitment to women's empowerment is highlighted by making Triple Talaq illegal and reserving one-third of legislative seats for women.

Cervical cancer, which develops in a woman's cervix, is the second-most common cancer among women in India. It is caused by persistent infection by the human papillomavirus (HPV). India accounts for nearly a quarter of all cervical cancer deaths in the world.

- **Health Sector:** The interim Budget announced the government's plans to focus on vaccination against **cervical cancer** for girls aged 9 to 14.
- **Other health-related schemes in her speech, including:**
  - The **U-WIN platform** for managing immunisations will be rolled out in the country.
  - **Extension of Ayushman Bharat Coverage:** The government will extend Ayushman Bharat cover to all Asha workers and Anganwadi workers and helpers.
  - **Expansion of Medical Colleges**: The government will focus on setting up more medical colleges by utilising existing hospital infrastructure in the country.
  - **Umbrella Scheme:** Schemes under maternal and child health care will be brought under one comprehensive programme.
  - An upgradation has also been announced of Anganwadi centres and expedited nutrition delivery and other steps for early childhood care.

> The term 'Lakhpati Didis' refers to women members of **Self-Help Groups (SHGs)** who harness their entrepreneurial skills and earn a sustainable income of at least ₹ 1 lakh per year per household.

- **'Lakhpati Didi' Scheme:** The government announced **that eighty-three lakh SHGs (self-help groups)** with **9 crore women** are transforming the rural socio-economic landscape with empowerment and self-reliance. Their success has assisted nearly one crore women to become **'Lakhpati Didi' already**. Buoyed by the success, it has been decided to enhance the target for 'Lakhpati Didi' from 2 crore to 3 crore.

> **Impact:**
>
> - The Lakhpati Didi Scheme, aiming to empower two crore women in villages, has achieved notable success by reaching 83 lakh self-help groups and benefiting 9 crore women.

- With a financial injection of **₹1 lakh per household** for one crore beneficiaries, this initiative is poised to significantly uplift the economic status of rural women.
- This empowerment will:
  - stimulate the rural economy
  - enhance credit demand for micro-financiers, particularly from women and self-help groups
  - reduce stress on asset quality issues

Investment

- The **FDI inflow** during 2014-23 was $596 billion marking a golden era. That is twice the inflow during 2005-14.
- For encouraging sustained foreign investment, the government is negotiating **bilateral investment treaties** with foreign partners, in the spirit of **'first develop India'.**

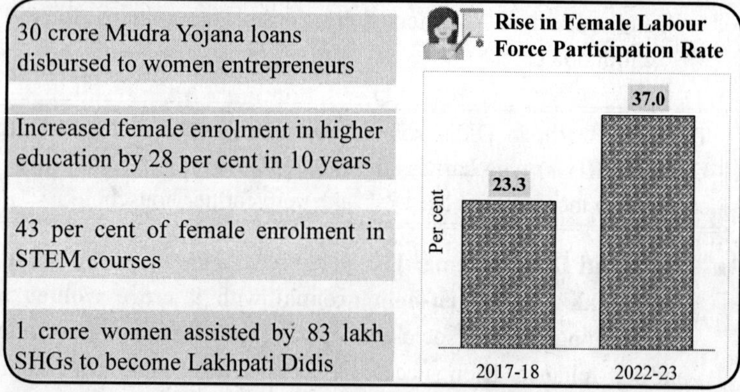

Tourism:

- **Interest free loans:** Long-term interest free loans would be given to various states to develop tourist centers, while highlighting that spiritual tourism saw a boost last year.
  - As much as **750 billion rupees at a 50-year interest free loan** will be set aside for states to boost tourism.

- **Rating system:** A rating system based on the quality of facilities and services will be established.
- **Lakshadweep Plan:** Projects for port connectivity, tourism infrastructure, and amenities will be taken up on islands, including Lakshadweep. This will help in generating employment as well.

> - **Travel and tourism** are two of the largest industries in India, with a total contribution of about US$ 178 billion to the country's GDP.
> - **Schemes:** PRASHAD, Swadesh Darshan, SAATHI, Dekho Apna Desh and NIDHI.

New Innovation Fund (Technology)

- New-age technologies is enabling new economic opportunities and facilitating the provision of high-quality services at affordable prices for all, including those at the 'bottom of the pyramid'.

The government plans to set up a ₹ 1 lakh crore corpus to back innovation. This includes 50-year interest-free loan, **long-term financing or refinancing** with long tenures with low or nil interest rates. The move is aimed at encouraging the private sector to scale up research and innovations **"significantly in sunrise domains".**

> **Impact:** This will encourage the private sector to scale up research and innovation significantly in sunrise domains.

OTHER IMPORTANT ANNOUNCEMENTS

- **Aqua Parks and Economic Corridor**: Five integrated Aqua Parks are slated to be established, promising recreational spaces for communities. Additionally, the recently announced India **Middle East Europe Economic Corridor** is expected to be a game-changer for India's economic landscape.

> **Middle East Europe Economic Corridor**
>
> - The project is a part of the **Partnership for Global Infrastructure Investment (PGII)** — a West-led initiative for **funding infrastructure projects** across the world.

- **Objective**: The corridor aims to provide a reliable and cost-effective **ship-to-rail transit network** between **Asia, Middle East and Europe.**
- **Proposals**: The corridor will comprise of **two separate corridors,**
  - **The Eastern corridor** - will connect India to the Arabian Gulf.
  - **The Northern corridor**- will connect the Arabian Gulf to Europe.
- **Member Nations**: Apart from India, the other participants will include **Saudi Arabia, UAE, France, Germany, Italy, USA and the European Union.**
- **Components of the project:**
  - The arrangement will include a **railway route** that, upon completion, will provide a **reliable and cost-effective cross-border ship-to-rail transit network** to supplement **existing maritime and road transport routes.**
  - This will enable **goods and services** to transit to, from, and between **India, the UAE, Saudi Arabia, Jordan, Israel, and Europe**.
  - Along the railway track, the members want to lay a **cable for clean hydrogen export**.

- **Bond sale programme:** The government announced a lower-than-expected bond sales programme for the next fiscal year, as the nation prepares for big foreign inflows on **global index inclusion.**

Government Bond Index-Emerging Markets index

- In 2023, **JP Morgan** announced that Indian government bonds will be included in its **Government Bond Index-Emerging Markets index** suite starting June 2024.
- The **JP Morgan GBI-EM** is a widely followed and influential benchmark index that tracks the performance of **local-currency-denominated Sovereign Bonds** issued by emerging market countries.

- **FDI Focus:** The government is set to push for bilateral treaties with foreign partners under the mantra of 'First Develop India,' promoting foreign direct investment.

HOW INDIA IS HANDLING THE GLOBAL SITUATION?

- The global situation is becoming more complex and challenging due to wars and conflicts in different parts of the world.
- Disruption of global supply chain (impacted trade): Russia-Ukraine conflict and the Israel-Hamas war.
- However, India has successfully navigated the global challenges in fuel and fertiliser price spike.
- India successfully navigated complex global affairs post-Covid, assuming the G20 summit leadership, being the "Vishwaguru" during challenging times.

SUCCESS STORIES

- The FM made some announcements that will go on to benefit the sector both directly and indirectly:

At glance

- The government has brought **250 million people out of poverty** in 10 years
- **Crop insurance scheme** benefits will reach 40 million farmers.
- **Inflation has moderated** and economic growth has picked up.
- Tax reforms have widened the tax base and **increased tax collections**
- **Average real income** of people increased by 50%.

- **Sabka Saath, Sabka Vikas:** A Decade of Poverty Alleviation Over the past decade, the government's commitment to "Sabka Saath" has resulted in 250 million people breaking free from multidimensional poverty, symbolizing inclusive development.

- **PM KISAN Yojana Success**: 118 million farmers have received financial assistance under the PM KISAN Yojana, marking a crucial step towards rural prosperity.
- **PM Awas Yojana (Gramin)** - Despite all the challenges, the implementation of this scheme continued, achieving the target of close to 3 crore houses and now aims for 2 crore more houses to be taken up in the next five years.
- **PM Mudra Yojana** has sanctioned 43 crore loans amounting to ₹ 22.5 lakh crore, fostering entrepreneurial aspirations. Additionally, Startup India and Startup Credit Guarantee Schemes are assisting the youth.
- **PM-SVANidhi** has provided credit assistance to 78 lakh street vendors.
- **Direct Transfer Impact**: Savings and Credit Assistance Direct transfers of ₹34 lakh crore through **PM Jan-Dhan** have led to significant government savings.
- **GST Success and Skill India Mission:** Over the last decade, the Indian economy has witnessed positive transformation, with moderate inflation and the successful implementation of GST. The Skill India Mission has trained and upskilled millions, establishing numerous educational institutions.
- **India's G20 Presidency Success**: Building Global Consensus India's successful G20 presidency showcased a forward-looking approach, building consensus on global solutions to challenges faced by the world.
- **Scaling new heights in sports:** The highest ever medal tally in **Asian Games and Asian Para Games in 2023** reflects a high confidence level. **Chess prodigy** and our **No. 1 ranked player Rameshbabu Praggnanandhaa** put up a stiff fight against the reigning **World Champion Magnus Carlsen** in 2023. Today, India has over 80 chess grandmasters compared to little over 20 in 2010

Important Schemes announced in Budget 2023

- **PM Vishwa Karma Kaushal Samman:** PM Vishwa Karma Kaushal Samman - package of assistance for traditional artisans and craftspeople has been conceptualised, will enable them to improve quality, scale & reach of their products, integrating with MSME value chain.

- **Free food scheme to continue till 2024:** From January 1, 2023, a scheme to supply free food grain to all **Antyodaya** and **priority households** for one year under **PM Garib Kalyan Ann Yojana** is underway.
- **Pradhan Mantri Awas Yojana:** The Budget 2023-24 allocated ₹ 79,000 crore for the Pradhan Mantri Awas Yojana (PMAY), giving a further boost to the government's programme to provide housing to the urban poor.
- **MISHTI scheme:** The government will take up mangrove plantations along the coastline under the new MISHTI scheme. The MISHTI scheme is aimed at preserving mangroves.
- **Atmanirbhar Clean Plant Programme**: The ₹2,200 crore programme to improve the availability of disease-free, quality planting material for high-value horticultural crops will raise their cultivation area from a low 15%.
- **Pradhan Mantri Kaushal Vikas Yojana 4.0:** The government will launch Pradhan Mantri Kaushal Vikas Yojana 4.0.
- **PM Azaz Yojana**: The outlay for PM Azaz Yojana is being increased by 66% to over ₹79,000 crore.
- **Amrit Dharohar:** The scheme aims to encourage optimal use of wetlands, and enhance bio-diversity, carbon stock, eco-tourism opportunities and income generation for local communities.
- **National Apprenticeship Promotion Scheme:** To provide stipend support to 47 lakh youth in three years, Direct Benefit Transfer under a pan-India National Apprenticeship Promotion Scheme will be rolled out.
- **National Financial Information Registry:** It will be set up to serve as the **central repository of financial and ancillary information**. This will facilitate efficient flow of credit, promote financial inclusion, and foster financial stability.
- **Azadi Ka Amrit Mahotsav Mahila Samman Bachat Patra:** For commemorating Azadi Ka Amrit Mahotsav, a one-time new small savings scheme, Mahila Samman Savings Certificate, will be made available for a two-year period up to March 2025.
- **PM Vishwakarma Kaushal Samman (PM VIKAS):** It is a package of assistance for traditional artisans and craftspeople. This will greatly benefit the Scheduled Castes, Scheduled Tribes, OBCs, women and people belonging to the weaker sections.

QUICK ANALYSIS

- **Tax:** The budget focused on **fiscal consolidation, infra, agri, green growth, and railways**. However, no changes were made in the tax rates, which was a disappointment to salaried individuals.
- **Industry status**: The industry has been requesting industry status for years, believing it would unlock benefits like easier access to credit, tax breaks, and infrastructure development. This wasn't explicitly addressed in the interim budget.
- **Tax benefits:** Tax incentives for homebuyers, such as increasing the deduction limit on home loan interest under Section 24, were expected. The interim budget remained silent on this as well.
- **Affordable housing**: Boosting allocations for schemes like PMAY (Urban) to improve affordability and encourage new projects in this segment was a key expectation. No major announcements appeared in the interim budget regarding this either.
- While the interim budget didn't directly address the real estate sector's key demands, the upcoming Union Budget might hold more concrete measures addressing industry concerns and potentially impacting market trends.
- The interim budget is seen as a stop-gap financial plan during an election year, aimed at meeting immediate financial needs before a new government is formed. The full-fledged Union Budget will only be released after the elections. The Budget has been touted as a roadmap to "vikshit Bharat", or developed India, by 2047.

PRELIMS MCQs

Q1: Consider the following statements about Inflation:

1. Headline Inflation measures the price rise in food, fuel and all other commodities.
2. Core Inflation does not consider inflation in fuel and food.

Which of the above statements is/are correct?

(a) Only 1 (b) Only 2

(c) Both 1 and 2 (d) Neither 1 nor 2

Q2: Consider the following statements regarding the measurement of the rate of inflation:

1. The rate of inflation is measured on the basis of the Wholesale Price Index (WPI) and Consumer Price Index (CPI).
2. A price index is a measure of the average level of prices.
3. Price index shows the exact price rise or fall of a single good.

Which of the following statements is/are correct?

(a) Only 1 (b) Both 1 and 2

(c) 2 and 3 (d) 1 and 3

Q3: What do you understand by the Inflationary gap?

(a) It is a situation which arises when Aggregate demand in the economy falls short of Aggregate Supply at the full employment level.

(b) It is a situation when inflation rises at an extremely faster rate.

(c) It is a situation which arises when Aggregate demand in an economy exceeds the Aggregate supply at the full employment level.

(d) The mechanism through which the central banks control inflation depends on interest rate.

Q4: Which of the following situations contribute to cause the Inflation situation in an economy?

1. Demand-supply gap
2. Excess circulation of money
3. Increase in tax rates

Select the correct answer using the codes given below:

(a) Only 1 (b) 1 and 2

(c) 2 and 3 (d) 1 and 3

Q5: With reference to the Finance Commission, consider the following statements:

1. The Constitution requires a Finance Commission (FC) to be set up every five years.
2. It is appointed by the President of India under Article 280 of the Constitution.
3. It recommends to the Prime Minister of India on the distribution of tax proceeds between the Union and the States.

Which of the statement(s) given above is/are correct?

(a) Only 1 (b) 1 and 2

(c) 2 and 3 (d) 1, 2 and 3

Q6: Which of the following statements is NOT correct regarding the Economic Survey of India?

(a) It presents detailed statistical data on different sectors.

(b) Projected Gross Domestic Product (GDP) growth constitutes a part of the Economic Survey.

(c) The finance ministry's chief economic adviser is in charge of preparing this document.

(d) The document is binding on the Government of India and must be applicable to Budget.

Q7: Consider the statements regarding Capital Expenditure:

1. It is the money spent by the government on the development of machinery, equipment, building, health facilities, education, etc.
2. It does not include the expenditure incurred on acquiring fixed assets.

Which of the statements given above is/are correct?

(a) Only 1 (b) Only 2

(c) Both 1 and 2 (d) Neither 1 nor 2

Q8: Consider the following pairs:

1. Net fiscal deficit: Gross fiscal deficit less net lending of the Central government.
2. Primary deficit: Difference between the government's income-expenditure gap and its interest payment on previous borrowings.
3. Effective revenue deficit: Difference between revenue deficit and grants for creation of capital assets.

Which of the above pairs is/are correctly matched?

(a) Only 1 (b) Only 2

(c) 2 and 3 (d) 1, 2 and 3

Q9: Consider the following:

1. Recovery of loans
2. State Provident Funds
3. Disinvestment proceeds
4. Treasury bills

Which of the above are the examples of non-debt capital receipts of the union government?

(a) 1, 2 and 4 only

(b) 2, 3 and 4 only

(c) 1 and 3 only

(d) 1, 3 and 4 only

Q10: Consider the following:

1. Fiscal Deficit
2. Gross Revenue Deficit
3. Receipts and Expenditures
4. Public Debt

How many of the above is/are broad aggregates of Budget?

(a) Only 1 (b) Only 2

(c) Only 3 (d) All 4

Q11: How many of the following illustrate the components of a Budget document?

1. Account of sources of receipts and their expenditure.
2. Details with respect to the resources transferred to the States and UTs.
3. Extracts of allocations for programme and schemes.
4. Sources of Deficit financing
5. Composition of variables allocated by the government

Select the correct option from the code given below:

(a) Only 2 (b) Only 3

(c) Only 4 (d) All 5

Q12: Which among the following reflects the 'Fiscal Deficit (FD)'?

(a) It is the total of the non-debt receipts and the total expenditure excluding revenue receipts.

(b) FD is reflective of the total borrowing requirement of Government.

(c) It is the difference between Revenue Deficit and Grant-in-Aid for Creation of Capital Assets.

(d) It is the primary deficit less interest payments.

Q13: Consider the following statements regarding expenditure estimations:

1. The total revenue expenditure during the FY 2023-24 is more than the actuals of FY 2022-23 by 2 crore approximately.

2. The effective capital expenditure has also been estimated with an increase of 17 % more than the revenue expenditure for FY 2023-24.

Which of the statements given above is/are correct?

(a) Only 1 (b) Only 2

(c) Both 1 and 2 (d) Neither 1 nor 2

Q14: Consider the following:

1. Grants and loans
2. Devolution of states
3. Funds under Centrally sponsored schemes
4. GST returns

How many of the above shows the union resources being transferred to states?

(a) Only 1 (b) Only 2

(c) Only 3 (d) All 4

Q15: Consider the following statements:

Statement I: The Revenue Expenditure for the year 2023-24 is reduced by ₹7151 crore on account of net amount payable by the Centre to the States for prior years.

Statement II: Nominal GDP for Budgetary Estimates 2024-25 has been assumed to grow by 10.5% as compared to the prior year's estimates.

Which one of the following is correct in respect of the above statements?

(a) Both Statement-I and Statement-II are correct, and Statement-II is the correct explanation for Statement-I.

(b) Both Statement-I and Statement-II are correct, and Statement-II is not the correct explanation for Statement-I.

(c) Statement I is correct, but Statement II is incorrect.

(d) Statement I is incorrect, but Statement II is correct.

Q16: Which among the following are sources of the government's income?

1. Corporation Tax
2. Borrowings and liabilities
3. Non-debt capital receipts
4. Non-tax receipts
5. Transfers
6. Subsidies

Select the correct option from the code given below:

(a) 1, 2, 3, 4 and 6 only (b) 2, 3, 4, 5 and 6 only
(c) 1, 2, 3, 4, and 5 only (d) 1, 2, 3 and 4 only

Q17: Consider the following:

1. Government securities (G-secs)
2. State Provident Funds
3. External debt
4. Long term borrowings

How many of the above is/are sources of Financing Fiscal Deficit?

(a) All 4 (b) Only 3
(c) Only 2 (d) Only 1

Q18: Consider the following statements:

Statement I: The Budget 2024-25 receipts estimation excludes recoveries of short-term loans and advances.

Statement II: The receipts are net of payment.

Which one of the following is correct in respect of the above statements?

(a) Both Statement-I and Statement-II are correct, and Statement-II is the correct explanation for Statement-I.
(b) Both Statement-I and Statement-II are correct, and Statement-II is not the correct explanation for Statement-I.
(c) Statement I is correct, but Statement II is incorrect.
(d) Statement I is incorrect, but Statement II is correct.

Q19: With respect to trends in net receipts of the centre, consider the following statements:

1. The centre's net tax revenue is six times as that of Non-tax revenue as per the budget estimates for FY 2024-25.
2. The share of non-debt capital receipts remains the highest amongst the net receipts sources.

Which of the statements given above is/are correct?

(a) Only 1 (b) Only 2

(c) Both 1 and 2 (d) Neither 1 nor 2

Q20: Consider the following statements:

1. As per the expenditure of the Union government, the share of centrally sponsored schemes is less than the central sector schemes.
2. The effective capital expenditure has been increased three times as compared to FY 2016-17.
3. Pension holds one of the highest shares of the government's expenditure calculations.

How many of the statements given above is/are incorrect?

(a) Only 1 (b) Only 2

(c) All 3 (d) None

Q21: Arrange the following in increasing order of the government's expenditure on major items during FY 2024-25:

(a) Defence < Energy < Health < Finance Rural Development

(b) Rural Development < Energy < Finance < Health < Defence

(c) Energy < Finance < Health < Rural Development < Defence

(d) Finance < Energy < Health < Rural Development < Defence

Q22: As per the budget estimates for 2024-25, the subsidy expenditure by the Government of India, Consider the following:

	Distribution of subsidy	**Share**
1.	Fertilizer	1.6 %
2.	Food	2.5 %
3.	Petroleum	4.09%

How many of then is/are correct?

(a) Only 1 (b) Only 2

(c) All 3 (d) None

Q23: Under PM-KISAN SAMMAN Yojana, consider the following statements:

1. It provides direct benefit transfer to small and marginal farmers.
2. The scheme is facilitated from farmer-centric policies to provide income support including coverage of risks through price.

Which of the statements given above is/are correct?

(a) Only 1 (b) Only 2

(c) Both 1 and 2 (d) Neither 1 nor 2

Q24: Consider the following statements:

Statement I: GIFT IFSC and the unified regulatory authority, IFSCA are creating a robust gateway for global capital and financial services for the economy.

Statement II: Digital Public Infrastructure is a new 'factor of production' in the 21st century and is instrumental in formalization of the economy.

Which one of the following is correct in respect of the above statements?

(a) Both Statement-I and Statement-II are correct, and Statement-II is the correct explanation for Statement-I.

(b) Both Statement-I and Statement-II are correct, and Statement-II is not the correct explanation for Statement-I.

(c) Statement I is correct, but Statement II is incorrect.

(d) Statement I is incorrect, but Statement II is correct

Q25: Regarding India's Global initiatives updated in recent times to expand the economy, consider the following statements:

1. The India-Middle East-Europe Economic Corridor was announced to reduce food, fertilizer, fuel, and finances for the world.

2. As per India, climate challenges are linked to very high public debt of the countries.
3. 'Viksit Bharat' aims of "Prosperous Bharat in harmony with nature, with modern infrastructure, and providing opportunities for all citizens".

How many of the above statements is/are correct?

(a) Only 1 (b) Only 2
(c) All 3 (d) None

Q26: With respect to the Government's commitment to Rooftop solarization, consider the following:

1. Through rooftop solarization, one crore households will be enabled to obtain up to 300 units free electricity every month.
2. Solar energy will save the surplus electricity and sold it to distribution companies.
3. It also aims to provide youth employment through technical training.
4. The electric vehicles infrastructure was also included under the solarisation programme.

How many of the statements given above is/are correct?

(a) Only 1 (b) Only 2
(c) Only 3 (d) All 4

Q27: Consider the following:

Initiatives	**Aim for**
U-WIN portal	Manage Immunisation of children
Saksham Anganwadi	Early childhood care
POSHAN 2.0	Improved nutrition delivery

How many of the above pair(s) is/are incorrect?

(a) Only 1 (b) Only 2
(c) All 3 (d) None

Q28: Consider the following statements with respect to dairy development in India:

Statement I: India is the world's largest milk producer but with low productivity of milch animals.

Statement II: Infrastructure Development Funds for dairy processing and animal husbandry aim to control foot and mouth disease in animals.

Which one of the following is correct in respect of the above statements?

(a) Both Statement-I and Statement-II are correct, and Statement-II is the correct explanation for Statement-I.

(b) Both Statement-I and Statement-II are correct, and Statement-II is not the correct explanation for Statement-I.

(c) Statement I is correct, but Statement II is incorrect.

(d) Statement I is incorrect, but Statement II is correct

Q29: Consider the following statements:

1. Bio-foundry schemes will provide environment friendly alternatives such as biodegradable polymers, bio-plastics, bio-pharmaceuticals and bio-agri-inputs.
2. This scheme will also help to shift towards consumptive manufacturing paradigm.

Which of the statements given above is/are correct?

(a) Only 1 (b) Only 2

(c) Both 1 and 2 (d) Neither 1 nor 2

Q30: Consider the following:

Statement I: Under the new tax scheme, the Government has reduced and rationalized tax rates.

Statement II: There is now no tax liability for taxpayers with income up to ₹ 10 lakhs.

Which one of the following is correct in respect of the above statements?

(a) Both Statement-I and Statement-II are correct, and Statement-II is the correct explanation for Statement-I.

(b) Both Statement-I and Statement-II are correct, and Statement-II is not the correct explanation for Statement-I.

(c) Statement I is correct, but Statement II is incorrect.

(d) Statement I is incorrect, but Statement II is correct

ANSWERS									
1. (c)	**2. (b)**	**3. (c)**	**4. (b)**	**5. (b)**	**6. (d)**	**7. (a)**	**8. (d)**	**9. (c)**	**10. (b)**
11. (d)	**12. (b)**	**13. (c)**	**14. (d)**	**15. (b)**	**16. (d)**	**17. (b)**	**18. (a)**	**19. (a)**	**20. (d)**
21. (c)	**22. (b)**	**23. (c)**	**24. (a)**	**25. (a)**	**26. (d)**	**27. (d)**	**28. (b)**	**29. (a)**	**30. (c)**

*****

MAINS PRACTICE QUESTIONS

Q1: The promotion of "Circular Economy" is key to sustainability. Analyse with examples.

Q2: Simplification of Tax regimes is vital to promote not only "Ease of Doing Business", but also "Ease of Living". Elucidate.

Q3: A challenge and incentive approach to various sectors can usher in much-needed competitive spirits for accelerated growth and development. Analyse.

Q4: Examine the importance of primary agricultural credit co-operatives and analyse the extent to which budgetary provisions to them would boost the agricultural sector.

Q5: Explain how start-up ecosystem in India will be boosted through the provisions of Union Budget converging priority sectors for inclusive and equitable economic growth?